TUTANKHAMEN
AND THE DISCOVERY
OF HIS TOMB

BY
G. ELLIOT SMITH

Routledge
Taylor & Francis Group

LONDON AND NEW YORK

First published in 2005 by Kegan Paul.

This edition first published in 2009 by
Routledge
2 Park Square, Milton Park, Abingdon, Oxon, OX14 4RN

Simultaneously published in the USA and Canada
by Routledge
711 Third Avenue, New York, NY 10017

First issued in paperback 2012

Routledge is an imprint of the Taylor & Francis Group, an informa business

British Library Cataloguing in Publication Data
A catalogue record for this book is available from the British Library

ISBN13: 978-0-415-65293-3 (pbk)
ISBN13: 978-0-710-31005-7 (hbk)

Publisher's Note
The publisher has gone to great lengths to ensure the quality of this reprint
but points out that some imperfections in the original copies may be
apparent. The publisher has made every effort to contact original copyright
holders and would welcome correspondence from those they have been
unable to trace.

CONTENTS

LIST OF ILLUSTRATIONS

PREFACE

DURING the period when the newspapers were publishing daily reports of the progress of the work in Tutankhamen's tomb and Mr Harry Burton's photographs, which gave us so vivid an impression of the objects that were being found, I wrote for the *Daily Telegraph* a series of articles discussing the wider signifi-cance of the startling discoveries. They did not describe the tomb itself or the wonderful collection of funerary equipment, but were merely a general commentary on the meaning of the information being given by the reporters from the Theban necropolis. Nor was any attempt made to collect the few facts concern-ing Tutankhamen himself, or even to discuss the events of his time. The exploration of the Valley of the Tombs of the Kings, for which the late Lord Carnarvon and Mr Howard Carter were responsible, had brought to light the tomb of the youthful nonentity Tutan-khamen, which sheds a dazzling searchlight on one particular phase of the history of civilization thirty centuries ago. What I set out to attempt was to interpret the deeper meaning of those Egyptian beliefs which found such brilliant expression in the luxuriously extravagant equipment of his tomb.

I have been urged to collect these articles into the more convenient form of this little book. As they were merely comments on the descriptions of the actual tomb and its contents the separate issue of these topical and ephemeral notes seemed at first to lack any justification, but I have received so many requests for information and guidance that I thought it might serve some useful purpose to redraft my articles and give such bibliographical references as would help the general reader to understand the results that have so far been attained and to appreciate the value of the more important discoveries that next season's work will certainly reveal.

I have used the pharaoh's name " Tutankhamen " as the title of this book merely as a label to suggest the circumstance that called it into being. But I have written an introductory chapter to give an account of what is known of him and his times.

BIBLIOGRAPHICAL NOTE

THE only accurate and reliable account that has ever been given of the Egyptian funerary practices and their significance is Dr Alan Gardiner's introductory memoir on *The Tomb of Amenemhēt* (illustrated by Nina de Garis Davies) which was published in 1915 under the auspices of the Egypt Exploration Fund (now Society).

Dr Gardiner describes the actual condition of affairs found in a private Theban tomb of the eighteenth dynasty (in the reign of Thothmes III, about a century earlier than Tutankhamen); and in the light of his intimate knowledge and understanding of the literature of the period, he interprets the meaning of the arrangement of the tomb and especially of the scenes and inscriptions sculptured and painted upon the walls, which Mrs de Garis Davies has reproduced with such skill and accuracy. This unique work is indispensable to anyone who wants to read what the ancient Egyptians themselves actually wrote to express their beliefs or interpret their customs. Professor James H. Breasted's *History of Egypt* and *Development of Religion and Thought in Ancient Egypt* are the best guides to a knowledge of the history and religion of ancient Egypt. The late Sir Gaston Maspero's *Egyptian Art* (London, 1913) contains a great deal of information directly relevant to the interpretation of objects in Tutankhamen's tomb. But Mr Burton's photographs of Tutankhamen's funerary equipment give a new interest and value to Birch's edition of Sir Gardner Wilkinson's *The Manners and Customs of the Ancient Egyptians* (London, 1878), for many of the objects and funeral scenes depicted in that remarkable book enable us to form a mental picture of the Valley of the Tombs as the funeral of Tutankhamen wound its way to the place where Mr Howard Carter has just brought to light so many articles closely analogous to those depicted in Birch's and Wilkinson's book.

All the information at present available concerning the life of Tutankhamen and Horemheb, his successor once removed, was collected and published (in 1912) by the late Sir Gaston Maspero, *The Tombs of Harmhabi*

*and Touatankhamanou (Theodore M. Davis'
Excavations).*

The other volumes of reports published by
Mr Theodore Davis are valuable for reference
and comparison in studying the results of the
exploration of Tutankhamen's tomb. The two
volumes, *The Tomb of Iouiya and Touiyou*
(1907) and *The Tomb of Queen Tiyi* (1910)
are specially important, and relevant to the
discoveries in Tutankhamen's tomb. Mr
Arthur Weigall's book *The Life and Times
of Akhanaton* gives a popular and romantic
picture of his conception of the history of
the times of Tutankhamen and his father-
in-law.

TUTANKHAMEN

CHAPTER I

NEVER before in the history of archæological inquiry has any event excited such immediate and world-wide interest as Mr Howard Carter's discovery of Tutankhamen's tomb in November 1922. Very little is known as yet of the king himself, but twelve months hence no doubt his mummy will give up its secrets and perhaps the story of his life will be revealed. But at the moment he is supposed to have been merely a colourless youth, who reigned for a few years only, and achieved such notoriety as is associated with his name by virtue of weakness rather than strength of character. For his religious and political opinions seem to have been as plastic as those of the famous Vicar of Bray, adapting themselves with facility to his changing environment. The objects so far found in his tomb do not add very materially to our knowledge of history.

Yet, in spite of the unimportance of Tutankhamen himself and the comparative lack of new historical data, the world-wide interest the discovery has evoked is amply warranted by the new appreciation of historical values it affords.

It gives us a new revelation of the wealth and luxury of Egyptian civilization during its most magnificent period. The value of the gold and precious objects far surpasses that of any hoard previously recovered from ancient times. Judged merely by its quantity the collection of furniture is the most wonderful ever found ; and everyone who has examined the individual pieces agrees that in beauty of design and perfection of craftsmanship Tutankhamen's funerary equipment is indeed a new revelation of the ancient Egyptians' artistic feeling and technical skill, far surpassing anything known before.

The fact that the tomb of so insignificant a personage as Tutankhamen was equipped with such lavish magnificence adds to the importance of the discovery. For if a youthful nonentity who reigned no more than six or seven years in one of the leanest phases of Egypt's history had all this wealth poured into his tomb, one's imagination tries in vain to picture the funerary equipment of the famous and longer-lived pharaohs, such as Thothmes III, who established the Egyptian Empire in Asia and could command the tribute of the then civilized world, or Amenhotep III, under whom the sovereign power in Egypt attained its culmination, and luxury and ostentation their fullest expression. Or again what riches must have been poured into the vast tombs of Seti I and Rameses II, the powerful pharaohs who recovered for a time the Egyptian dominion in Asia which Akhenaton and his sons-in-law had lost? A thousand years before Christ the desolate Valley of the Tombs of the Kings must have had buried in its recesses the vastest collection of gold and precious furniture that perhaps was ever collected in one spot in the history of the world. For these reasons alone there is ample justification for the world-wide interest in the discovery which will always be associated with the names of Lord Carnarvon and Mr Howard Carter.

But apart from its interest as an artistic revelation and the intrinsic value of the objects found the discovery is important for other reasons. The dazzling display of skill and luxury has forced the scholar and the man in the

street to recognize in some measure the vast-
ness of the achievements of ancient Egyptian
civilization and to ask themselves whether this
vigorous and highly developed culture could
have failed to exert a much more profound
influence upon its neighbours than is generally
admitted. When it is recalled that Egypt
herself devised the ships and developed the
seamanship which created the chief bond of
union with Syria and Crete, East Africa and
Arabia, the Persian Gulf and beyond, we
should be in a better position to realize the
plain meaning of the evidence that points to
Egypt as the dominating factor in shaping the
nascent civilization of the world. The wide
interest in the revelation of Egypt's achievements more than thirty centuries ago should
prepare men's minds impartially to study the
vast significance of the facts thus displayed by
Mr Howard Carter's investigations.

Besides revealing the wonderful equipment of
a royal tomb the discovery of Tutankhamen's
tomb enables us to examine many objects and
articles of funerary equipment hitherto known
to us only in pictures. This makes it possible
for us not only to study and appreciate the
nature of the things themselves, but also to
acquire new confidence in the accuracy and the

reality of the scenes and the objects depicted upon the walls of the tombs and the pictures inscribed on papyri. Many of the illustrations that have long been familiar to us in the old books of Belzoni, Lepsius, Rosellini, and Wilkinson, have acquired a new meaning and a new reality from the discovery of Tutankhamen's tomb. Moreover, when the examination of the tomb is completed, and we learn something of the mummy, the king's distinctive features, his age, and his ailments, we shall be able to read the history of his time more clearly, and perhaps be able to appreciate the deeper significance of one of the most piquant phases in the history of civilization.

At the time of Tutankhamen the great peoples that had built up civilization were losing their dominant position. Egypt's power was showing definite signs of weakness, which were intensified rather than caused solely by the pacifist policy of Akhenaton and his sons-in-law. For even the vigorous rule of the powerful pharaohs of the nineteenth dynasty merely revived Egyptian power for a time before its final collapse. Fifty years before Tutankhamen, the Palace of Knossos had been destroyed in Crete, marking the downfall of the great pioneer of Mediterranean civilization to which Greece and Europe as a whole became heir. Babylonia also had reached the limits of her influence: and the weakening of these three earliest great powers allowed the Hittites and the Assyrians to struggle the one with the other for supremacy, crushing out such states as that of the Mitanni, and by exhausting themselves, so prepared the way for the eventual incursion of Persia into the Mediterranean area.

Another reason why the sudden weakening of Egyptian influence in Asia under Akhenaton and Tutankhamen is so important an event in the history of civilization is because it occurred at a time when the literature of the Jews was becoming crystallized in the shape that was destined to exert so tremendous an influence upon the history of belief and social practice. If Egyptian rule had not been weakened at this particular time and Palestine had not been subjected to the disturbing influences of Syrian, Hittite, and Assyrian interference, the Old Testament would not have been composed in the atmosphere of strife that gives it its distinctive tone and seems to us to-day unduly to exalt the importance of warfare and the value of military courage.

But if the weakness of Akhenaton and

Tutankhamen contributed in some measure to the facilitation of strife in Palestine and its reaction upon the sacred literature of the world, the times in which these events occurred were pregnant with new trends in the development of civilization for which these weak kinglets could not be held responsible. Aryan-speaking people had recently made their appearance on the stage of history for the first time, in Asia Minor and around the head waters of the Euphrates in Syria, and in the approaching disruption of the powers of Western Asia, the influence of these people of Indo-European speech was destined to make itself obtrusive in Persia and India and exert a growing influence upon religious beliefs and social practices.

But simultaneously with these events of far-reaching significance in Asia, the people of Europe also first intruded upon the attention of Egypt, and revealed the fact that a new orientation of political influence was in preparation.

Between Asia and Europe the disturbances in the Levant played some part in launching upon their world-wide career of exploitation the persistent trading people we know as Phœnicians, who were responsible for the

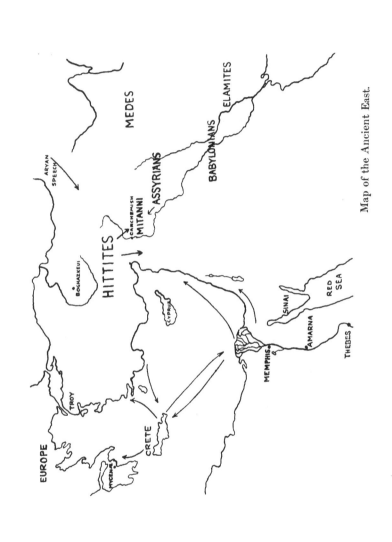

Map of the Ancient East.

rapid diffusion of the elements of civilization during several centuries from Tutankhamen's time onward. At the moment it is the fashion to scoff at the Phœnicians and their works : but no one who seriously studies the evidence relating to their achievements is likely to be deceived by this pose. For there is no doubt these people did fulfil the rôle attributed to them in the Book of Ezekiel.

The period which is so brilliantly illuminated by the discovery of Tutankhamen's tomb is thus perhaps the most critical period in the whole history of civilization. A new era was dawning and every scrap of information that sheds any light upon the circumstances of this fateful time is of tremendous interest to us in understanding the civilization under which we ourselves are living.

CHAPTER II

THE work of modern exploration of the Valley
of the Tombs of the Kings can be said to have
begun in 1819 when the traveller Belzoni
opened and wrote a description of the tomb
of Seti I. In 1881 the discovery was made
of a collection of royal mummies, many of
which had been buried about thirty centuries
ago in the Valley of the Tombs, and had been
removed about 1000 B.C. and hidden in a
chamber in the great cliff (behind Deir el
Bahari) that faces the Nile across the Theban
plain. This stimulated renewed interest in
the famous necropolis, but it was not until
1898 that the work of exploration there was
rewarded by the discovery of the tomb of
Amenhotep II containing the mummy of that
pharaoh himself —the only king's mummy ever
found in his own tomb before the discovery
of Tutankhamen's, in which it is confidently

believed the mummy is present and undisturbed, an unprecedented circumstance which will make the investigations next winter peculiarly important. For the mummy of Amenhotep II had been badly plundered like all those discovered before or since until the opening of Tutankhamen's burial chamber made it practically certain that in it will be revealed for the first time to modern men the undisturbed tomb of an ancient Egyptian king.

When Mr Howard Carter was appointed Chief Inspector of Antiquities for Upper Egypt his chief function was to safeguard the antiquities in the Thebaid. The Egyptian Government through its Archæological Committee has been in the habit (until the present year, when the wise rule that encouraged serious archæological exploration is being revoked) of granting to archæologists whose competence was regarded as satisfactory permission to excavate on ancient sites, and the Antiquities Department allowed such workers to take out of the country half the antiquities brought to light. But the Valley of the Tombs of the Kings was excluded from the operation of this rule, because the Antiquities Department reserved for itself a site of such historical importance. Hence when Mr Howard Carter

C

took charge of the Theban inspectorate he was in a serious dilemma. The deserted Valley of the Tombs of the Kings, in the hidden depths of which was hoarded the remains of the vastest collection of valuable antiquities ever assembled, was in his charge, and alongside it the modern population of Luxor and Sheikh abd-el-Gournah, the most skilful and persistent group of tomb-robbers who had been habituated to the practice of this craft for many centuries. Yet he could not solve the difficulty by the most efficient form of control, that is, by carrying on excavations there, because the Antiquities Department had no funds for such work and, for the reasons already given, private excavators were not allowed to work in the Valley of the Tombs. Mr Carter was fortunate in being able to find a solution of the problem that evaded all these difficulties. Mr Theodore M. Davis, of Newport, Rhode Island, who was visiting Egypt as a tourist in the winter 1902-1903, was persuaded to place at the disposal of the Department of Antiquities the funds for exploration in the Valley of the Tombs without claiming any reward beyond the kudos which his action brought. Hence in 1903 Mr Howard Carter began excavating in the Valley at Mr Davis's expense and discovered the tomb of Thothmes IV. The mummy of this pharaoh, which had

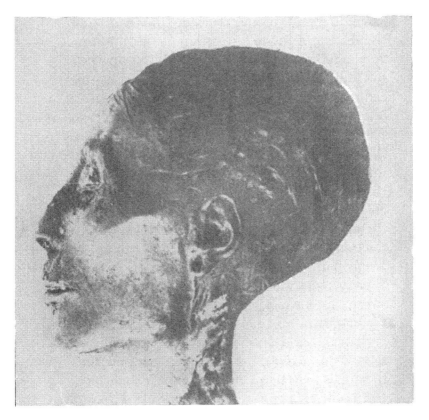

Fig. 1.—Mummy of Thothmes IV.

been found in 1898 by M. Loret in the tomb of Amenhotep II, was unwrapped after its original tomb was found; and at Mr Carter's suggestion, M. Maspero asked me to investigate it. Mr Davis published a magnificent volume giving a report of the work in the tomb and the results of the investigation of the mummy. In the following years the expedition financed by Mr Davis found six other important inscribed tombs, those of Queen Hatshepsut, Yuaa and Tuaa (the parents of Queen Tiy), King Siptah, Prince Mentuherkhepshef, King Akhenaton and King Horemheb, and nine uninscribed tombs, one of which contained the beautiful gold jewellery of Queen Tausret and of her second husband Seti II, and another the pieces of inscribed gold plate stolen during the reign of Horemheb from the tombs of Kings Tutankhamen and Ay.

Before the war Mr Davis had completed his share of the work. He imagined that he had found the tomb of Tutankhamen, and in the preface of the last of his series of magnificent reports he makes the remark: " I fear that the Valley of the Tombs is now exhausted." But it is a fortunate thing that Mr Howard Carter did not share this idea. After the war the late Lord Carnarvon, with whom Mr Howard Carter had been working since 1907, applied to the Antiquities Department, and was granted a concession to be allowed to continue in the Valley of the Tombs the work which the late Mr Theodore Davis had abandoned. The work carried out by Lord Carnarvon and Mr Howard Carter before they took over Mr Davis's concession led to some important discoveries, the chief results of which were published in 1912, in a magnificent volume *Five Years' Exploration at Thebes*.

In the Valley of the Tombs of the Kings they carried out real and thorough exploration, as no previous workers had done. Instead of making mere exploratory openings into the masses of rubble they began systematically to clear the ground, moving vast quantities of material—they are said to have moved as much as 200,000 tons in the process. In spite of the discouragement of doing work of so exhaustive and expensive a kind with no further reward than a few unimportant pots, they pressed on, until on 5th November 1922 their indomitable persistence was rewarded with the most wonderful discovery ever made in the history of archæological investigation.

The day before he left London last January to return to Egypt Lord Carnarvon gave this account of the discovery. In the famous tomb of the Vizier Rekhmara no burial shaft could be found, and after searching for it near the tomb-building it was decided to try in the Valley of the Tombs. While cleaning the floor of the valley for this purpose, Mr Carter found a step cut in the rock and after further clearance he found a wall in the cement upon which was impressed the seal of the Royal Necropolis. Further examination revealed the presence of a tomb that had been entered soon after the burial. It bore the cartouche of the King Tutankhamen.

The story of the amazing treasures that have so far been discovered in the tomb has been told in the daily press day by day from November 1922 until April 1923, and Mr Harry Burton's photographs have given us a realistic idea of their appearance.

The plan of the tomb presents a marked contrast to the more familiar Theban burial places; but it becomes more intelligible when it is compared with those which were made at the heretic king's capital during the time of Akhenaton.

Of the four chambers in the tomb only one has up to now so far been examined, and when the inventory comes to be made of the annexe, which is now packed with furniture, and the room leading out of the burial chamber, the largest and most wonderful collection of ancient furniture that has ever been made will be revealed.

But the most marvellous revelations of all await the investigator next season when the shrines in the burial chamber are opened and the sarcophagus and the coffins within it are made to reveal to us how a royal mummy was prepared for its eternal home.

The plan of the tomb of Rameses IV, made more than two centuries later than the time of Tutankhamen, is the only evidence we have of the arrangement of the coffins within the shrines; but the coffins of Yuaa and Tuaa, the great-grandparents of Tutankhamen's wife, and especially the wonderful coffin made for Akhenaton, his father-in-law, have prepared us for what we are to find next winter. But the artistic inspiration revealed in the design of Tutankhamen's funerary furniture and the craftsmanship are so vastly superior to those displayed in other tombs that we cannot predict what gems of art will be found when the inner coffins are exposed.

Of the mummy itself we can predict the success of the embalmer's efforts, because the art of preserving the body was at its best in the period from Amenhotep II until

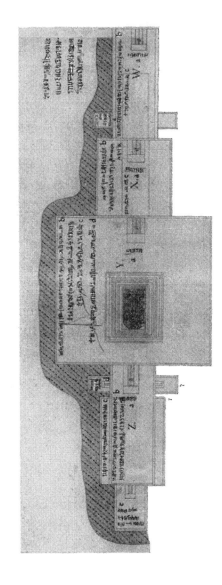

FIG. 2.—Ancient Plan of the Tomb of Rameses IV with an interpretation by Howard Carter and Alan Gardiner (*Journal of Egyptian Archæology*).

Fig. 3.—The Mummies of Yuaa and Tuaa, the latest complete
mummies known before the time of Tutankhamen, and the
mummy of Seti I, the earliest after him. These mummies
will give some idea of the state of preservation likely to be
revealed in Tutankhamen's mummy.

Rameses II, but some very interesting points in the technique of embalming remain to be discovered. In the case of Amenhotep III, the latest mummy of the eighteenth dynasty so far examined, the new procedure for stuffing packing material under the skin was introduced for the first time. In the nineteenth and twentieth dynasties it was completely given up, only to be readopted in the twenty-first dynasty. It will be interesting to discover whether or not this procedure was still in vogue at the time of Tutankhamen.

The most interesting discovery of all that next season holds in store will be the equipment of jewellery with which the mummy will be provided. So far all that we know of such jewels has been derived from the recovery of odd fragments and the impressions left upon the mummy's wrappings by the pieces long since stolen.

CHAPTER III

DURING the course of the excavations in the Valley of the Tombs of the Kings made on behalf of the late Mr Theodore M. Davis in the years 1906 and 1907, a series of objects were discovered bearing the name of Tutankhamen. In all probability they were stolen from his tomb during the reign of Horemheb, only a few years after the pharaoh was buried.

Under a large rock, found tilted on one side near the foot of a high hill, the late Mr Edward Ayrton, who was in charge of Mr Davis's Exploration in 1906, found a beautiful blue glaze cup bearing the cartouche of Tutankhamen. In the following year, when the late Mr E. Harold Jones was superintending the work, a rock-cut chamber was found; and as it contained so many objects bearing the name of Tutankhamen it was assumed by Mr Davis that he had discovered that king's tomb. Hence the

volume published in 1912 giving an account
of the work of 1906, 1907, and 1908 (during
the last of which the tomb of Horemheb
was found on the south side of the chamber
already mentioned) was entitled *The Tombs of
Harmhabi* [Horemheb] *and Touatânkhamanou*
[Tutankhamen] (Theodore M. Davis' Excavations: Bibân el Molük), and the late Sir
Gaston Maspero gave accounts of all that was
then known of the lives of both Horemheb
and Tutankhamen. It is only right to add
that Sir Gaston Maspero did not regard the
chamber opened by Mr Harold Jones as the
tomb of Tutankhamen. For in the closing
paragraph of his report on the scanty information we have of Tutankhamen's life and
achievements, he states: " I suppose his tomb
was in the Western Valley, somewhere between
or near Amenôthes III [Amenhotep III,
the last royal mummy known to have been
buried at Thebes before Tutankhamen, because
Akhenaton and Smenkhara were buried at
El Amarna, and removed to Thebes later] and
Aiya [Ay, the successor of Tutankhamen]:
when the reaction against Atonu and his
followers was complete, his mummy and his
furniture were .taken to a hiding - place, as
those of Tiyi and Khuniatonu had been,

probably under Harmhabi, and there Davis found what remained of it after so many transfers and plunders. But this also is a mere hypothesis, the truth of which we have no means of proving or disproving as yet."

Although Sir Gaston was right in assuming that the chamber discovered in 1907 was not Tutankhamen's tomb, his hypothesis that the latter might have been in the neighbourhood of his predecessor (Amenhotep III) and his successor (Ay) has been shown by Mr Howard Carter's recent discovery not to be true. The chamber seems to have been nothing more than a safe (perhaps cut out by the workmen who were making a tomb for Horemheb) in which plunderers of the tombs of Tutankhamen and Ay hid their spoil. Why they were unable to rescue all the gold they stole and so hid away is not apparent. The chamber was buried at a depth of 25 feet and was almost filled with mud, which had been swept into it by the rain of many centuries. In this room was found a broken box containing several pieces of gold stamped with the names of Tutankhamen and his wife Ankhsenamen, and others bearing the name of his successor called the King's Father-in-law Ay and his wife Tiy, but without any title or prenomen. In the mud was found the very beautiful statuette made of fine translucent aragonite commonly called "alabaster." Apart from its value as a wonderful work of art this figure is interesting as the broad scarf around the loins is tied in the Syrian fashion. Unfortunately there is no inscription on it. M. Daressy makes the tentative suggestion that it may represent Ay before his succession to the throne.

When it is recalled that in the recently discovered tomb parts of the gold plating were found to have been torn off the throne and other pieces of furniture brought to light by Lord Carnarvon's expedition, it is interesting to note that the inscribed sheets of gold found in 1908 represent scenes of Tutankhamen's triumphs and captured prisoners such as would have adorned the tomb furniture that has been found mutilated. Other pieces of gold represent similar scenes from furniture plundered from the tomb of Tutankhamen's successor Ay.

A few days after the discovery of the chamber containing these stolen objects a pit was found, some distance away from it, in which there were large earthenware pots containing debris from a tomb, such as wreaths of leaves and flowers and small bags of powdered substance. The cover of one of these jars was broken and wrapped around it was a piece of linen bearing an inscription in ink which refers to the sixth year of Tutankhamen's reign.

In this volume, as I have already mentioned, the late Sir Gaston Maspero collected together the few scraps of information available in 1912 with reference to the life and reign of Tutankhamen.

In the British Museum there are two models of lions sculptured from red granite, one of which was made at the instigation of Amenhotep III for a temple in the Soudan. The other one may have been carved for Tutankhamen, who claims that he " repaired the monuments of his father Amenhotep." For nearly a century scholars have been discussing the question whether the use of the word " father " was intended to refer to his parentage, whether, in fact, Tutankhamen was a brother or half-brother of his father-in-law the heretic king Akhenaton, or whether the word was used simply as a term of respect for his predecessor. The problem still remains unsolved, for Tutankhamen's elevation to the throne was due to his marriage with the daughter of Akhenaton, the customary method in ancient Egypt for establishing a right to the kingship.

Fig. 4.—Tutankhamen receiving Ethiopian tribute from Huy.
[*After Lepsius.*

At the time of his marriage and succession he belonged to the Aton faith, which his father-in-law had established, and his name was Tutankhaton. But as soon as Akhenaton died, Tutankhaton and his wife Ankhsenpaaton abandoned the heresy and returned to the orthodox faith of Amen. As a token of their conversion they changed their names to Tutankhamen and Ankhsenamen and left Akhenaton's capital for Thebes, the headquarters of the priesthood of Amen, who no doubt were responsible for Tutankhamen's sudden return to the old religion.

The little information we possess of his reign is derived mainly from the inscriptions upon the Theban temples restored by him after his return to the orthodox faith, though many of these records are palimpsests, for Horemheb replaced Tutankhamen's name on most of them. The two other chief sources of information are : (*a*) the piece of linen found in 1907, which is the only certain evidence that he reigned as long as six years ; and (*b*) a remarkably interesting series of wall-pictures in the tombs of Huy at Kurnet (Murrai), which afford the only record we have of Tutankhamen's relations with Ethiopia and Asia. These pictures are among the most

D

FIG. 5.—Part of the Asiatic tribute presented to Tutankhamen
by Huy. [*After Lepsius.*

familiar records of ancient Egyptian life, having been used by Champollion, Lepsius, Brugsch and Piehl, and the inscriptions describing the scenes have been translated into English by Professor Breasted.[1]

[1] *Ancient Records of Egypt*, Vol. II. pp. 420-427.

CHAPTER IV

THE SIGNIFICANCE OF THE DISCOVERY

WHEN the eyes of all the world are focussed on the tomb of Tutankhamen and the fresh revelation it affords of the superb achievements of the ancient Egyptians in the arts and crafts, it is worth while to consider how this new discovery is likely to affect our attitude to the history of civilization and to promote a fuller recognition of the human motives that found expression in its creation and development. Apart from the demonstration it affords of the fabulous wealth that was hidden away more than thirty centuries ago in the Valley of the Tombs of the Kings, the new discovery appeals as an æsthetic revelation of dazzling brilliance rather than as an addition to our knowledge. So far its effect has been to force the scholar and the man in the street to take an interest in the civilization that was capable of producing such perfect works of art, and to ask themselves whether this precocious culture was really so exotic as it is commonly supposed to have been, or whether, on the contrary, such achievements on the very threshold of a yet un-enlightened Europe did not exert a far greater influence than it is usual to accord them.

But at present we are concerned simply in considering what is the significance of the dis-coveries so far made ; the furniture, which has never been surpassed in the perfection of its workmanship and exquisite decoration ; linen of a fineness and a beauty of texture that have never been excelled ; carved alabaster vases such as the world has never seen before ; and statues that afford some justification for the ancient belief that they were, in truth, " living images." What is the meaning of all this lavish display of skill and beauty ? Why was so much wealth poured into the hidden recesses of this desolate ravine, and the most exquisite products of the world's achievement in the arts and crafts buried out of sight in this strange necropolis ? The true answers to these questions reveal the motive force that brought about the development of civilization and made Egypt the pioneer in its creation.

Embalming and Immortality

All these elaborate preparations, the laborious and costly process of hewing the tomb out of

the solid rock and furnishing it with such
magnificence, were made because the ancient
Egyptians believed that the king's body to
be housed in it had been made imperishable.
They imagined that when the body was embalmed the continuation of the king's existence
had been assured.   Hence they provided him
with food and raiment, the furniture and
amulets, the jewels and the unguents, and
other luxuries which he had been accustomed
to enjoy, before he was taken to his " eternal
house " in the desolate Valley of the Tombs.
There can be no doubt that in the early days
of Egyptian history this naïve belief was
regarded in all seriousness as the simple truth.
In fact, the thoroughness with which at first
the Egyptians gave concrete expression to
their faith in making material provision for
every want that the deceased might experience
could only have been inspired by the confidence that all these preparations were indeed
effective.   This conviction was deeply rooted
in the practice of mummifying the dead,
preserving the body so that it should become
incorruptible and everlasting ; and this was
supposed also to involve the feasibility of the
prolongation of the dead man's existence.

The hope of survival was thus based upon

the efficacy of the embalmer's art; and the
extraordinary constancy with which for more
than thirty centuries—for a span of years four
times the length of time that separates us
from the arrival of William the Conqueror in
Britain—they persisted in their efforts to
improve their methods and render more
perfect this gruesome practice is a striking
tribute to the fundamental importance of
mummification to the Egyptians. The craft
of the carpenter was first invented for the
manufacture of coffins to protect the corpse;
the stonemason's first experiments had for
their aim the preparation of rock-cut chambers
still further to ensure its safety: the first
buildings worthy of being called architecture
were intended to promote the welfare of the
dead, to provide places to which relatives
could bring food necessary for the dead man's
sustenance, and a room to house his portrait
statue—another art that was the outcome of
the practice of mummification—which took
his place at the temple of offerings and preserved his likeness for all time.

These elements of civilization, the arts of
architecture and sculpture, and the crafts of
the carpenter and the stonemason, were thus
direct results of the custom of embalming.

But its influence in moulding ritual and belief
was no less profound and far-reaching.

Early Beliefs

The belief in the possibility of the continuation of existence after death may have been
(and probably was) much older than the
Egyptians; but the evidence now available
seems fairly decisive that the belief in immortality was not definitely formulated by mankind until the means had been devised of
making the corpse everlasting, when " the
corruptible body put on incorruption." Moreover, the ritual of the most primitive religions
was based upon the practices of the early
Egyptians for revivifying the mummy, or its
surrogate, the mortuary statue, by burning
incense, pouring out libations, opening its
mouth to give it the breath of life, and per-
forming a series of dramatic acts to animate it.
By means of these ritual procedures it was
supposed that the officiating priest was able
to restore consciousness to the dead body and
so make it possible for it not only to take an
intelligent share in the life around it, but also
to hear appeals for help and guidance and to
answer such requests.

Egypt alone of the countries of antiquity

provides the explanation of these strange beliefs and practices. They were devised by the concrete-minded people of the Nile Valley as part of a comprehensive philosophy of life and death which was formulated as a sort of life insurance, in accordance with the principles of which the deceased himself was supposed to be the beneficiary, and his reward an indefinite prolongation of existence.

This remarkable system of beliefs originated even before the beginning of civilization, sixty centuries ago; but the latter event was responsible for intensifying the conviction of its reality and increasing men's hope in its potency.

The Dawn of Civilization

Civilization began when the Egyptians first devised the methods of agriculture and invented a system of irrigation. The irrigation engineer was the first man in the history of the world to control and organize the co-operative work of his fellow-men, and become the ruler of a whole community. If there is one lesson more than another that history has demonstrated in Egypt, equally in ancient and in modern times, it is the absolute necessity of a strong and autocratic Government, because the conditions in the Nile Valley are such that the prosperity of the country and the welfare of the whole community is entirely dependent upon the just and equitable distribution of the waters of irrigation throughout the land. It is not to be wondered at that the engineer who successfully achieved this task, and in a very special and real sense controlled the lives and destinies of his people, became the king, whose beneficence was apotheosized after his death, so that he became the god Osiris, who was identified with the river, whose life-giving powers he controlled. For to a people who had never experienced anything of the kind before it must have seemed an altogether miraculous and superhuman act for one man to have in his absolute control the prosperity of a whole community and every individual unit of it.

The connection between this story and the tomb of Tutankhamen may not be apparent. But when it is realized that the original invention of the social system was so closely identified with the god Osiris, it will be understood that the ritual of mummification and burial aimed at identifying the deceased with Osiris, and by imitating the incidents of his story to secure for the deceased a fate

Fig. 6.—Part of a mace-head found by Mr J. E. Quibell at
Hierakonpolis in 1897-8, showing one of the earliest kings
of Egypt engaged in the task of cutting an irrigation canal.

like that of the god, whose life-giving powers were sought to grant the continuation of existence.

The early kings of Egypt, rich in their newly acquired control of the labour and wealth of their dominion, did not hesitate to squander both in the preparation of their tombs, in the vain belief that thereby they were making certain their own survival. Twenty centuries later, in the times of Tutankhamen, they were still obsessed with the same idea, and spent fabulous sums in preparing their tombs in the Biban el Moluk.

The peculiar importance of the study of these strange customs and beliefs in Egypt depends upon the fact that, not only were they invented by the Egyptians, and preserved in their entirety, so that the whole story of its development can be read in all their childish directness and simplicity, but also because other peoples of antiquity, to whose civilization Europe owes her own heritage, adopted some of the results of these Egyptian devices, and, after eliminating some of their cruder details, transformed them into the essentials of the world's civilization. Hence, in recovering the history of Egyptian cultural development, we are really probing into the sources of the customs and beliefs of

our own everyday life and experience.   Thus
we must regard mummification as something
more than an eccentric practice that excites
our curiosity.   For it played a fundamental
part in shaping the development of civilization,
both its arts and crafts, as well as its most
vital customs and beliefs.

Giving Life to the Dead

If we turn to consider the process of mummification, and the aims of its practitioners, it
will be found that throughout the long ages in
which it was in vogue the Egyptian embalmer
kept constantly striving to attain two aims.
His first object was to preserve the actual
tissues of the body as thoroughly as he could.
But he was also attempting the much more
difficult task of preserving the natural form of
the body, and especially of the features.   He
was prompted to make this effort, not merely
that the deceased should retain his distinctive
traits in a recognizable form, but rather that
the simulacrum should be the " living " image
of himself.   In other words, the aim was to
make the representation of the dead man so
life-like that he should, in fact, remain alive,
and be certain of maintaining his existence.

The early Egyptians seem to have entertained
in all its childlike *naïveté* the belief that
they were actually conferring vitality upon
the image when they made it life-like. The
Egyptian verb for describing the work of the
sculptor who carved the portrait statue meant
literally, according to Dr Alan Gardiner, "to
give birth," in the sense of "giving life"; and
there is no doubt they meant this idea of life-
giving to be accepted as the simple expression
of a fact, and not merely as a symbol or
analogy.

It must not be forgotten that when these
beliefs were first formulated, more than fifty
centuries ago, there was no knowledge or
understanding of the principles of physics and
biology to hinder the adoption of such naïve
fancies as the simple and obvious truth. There
is no reason to doubt that the philosophers of
those days did honestly believe in the possibility of prolonging existence by fulfilling all
the conditions that seemed to them essential
and adequate to the maintenance of vitality.

When mummification was first devised,
probably at the time of the earliest dynasty
(about 3400 B.C.) it was realized that if, in
the climate of Egypt, the preservation of the
tissues of the body was not very difficult to

effect, the task of retaining the distinctive features was practically unattainable. All kinds of devices were tried, during the second, third, and fourth dynasties, by wrapping the mummy so as to simulate the human form, painting it, applying clay or resinous paste, and modelling it into a portrait statue upon the enshrouded mummy itself. When these devices failed to achieve the desired aim of making life-like portraits, the art of modelling statues of the deceased in stone or wood was invented, and paint and artificial eyes were used to make them as life-like as possible. The skill with which the Egyptians of the Pyramid Age overcame the technical difficulties of the sculptors' art and made life-size portraits which, as I have said before, could not untruthfully be called " living images," is one of the most amazing achievements in the history of art. But it was more than the triumph of a craftsman : it was the realization of a deeper desire to preserve the image, and so prolong the existence of the sculptor's model, the deceased, who was thus supposed to have been saved from annihilation.

In the first chapter of my book *The Evolution of the Dragon*, I have discussed this problem more fully.

Fig. 7.—Portrait of Hesi, *circa* 3000 B.C., to show the skill displayed even at the beginning of Egyptian history in carving portraits in wood. As a rule they were made in the round and life size. This funerary portrait cut in low relief in wood is exceptional.

Success after Twenty Centuries

Although these early sculptors had achieved
so signal a triumph, the embalmers never

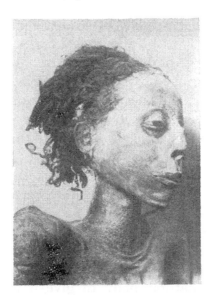

Fig. 8.—The " packed " mummy of a Queen of the
Twenty-first Dynasty.

abandoned the hope of bringing their art to
such a state of perfection as to make of the
mummy itself the simulacrum of the deceased.
With infinite patience and persistence they
experimented through one millennium after
another to attain this object.   But it was not

E

until the time of the twenty-first dynasty,
more than twenty centuries after they first
attempted to do it, that they were able to
transform the mummy itself into a portrait
statue. From the artistic point this represents
to us a debasement of æsthetic motive and
practice; but to the embalmer it was the
culmination of his achievement. But it was
also the prelude to the degradation of his art.
For the technique became so complex and
difficult of execution that failure became a
common incident, and to disguise the evidence
of such incompetence the practice grew up of
paying chief attention to the external appearance of the wrappings rather than to the
corpse.

But to us the complicated technique of the
embalmers during the twenty-first dynasty
appeals rather as ingenious trickery, a tampering
with the natural body to give it a spurious
and trumpery resemblance to a living being.
Judged by our artistic standards there can be
no doubt that the ancient Egyptian practice
of mummification was seen at its best at the
end of the eighteenth dynasty, that is about
the time of Tutankhamen. The most successful results are revealed in the mummies of
Yuaa and Tuaa and of Seti I (Fig. 3, p. 33),

which means that at the time when Tutankhamen was embalmed the craftsmen had the
skill and the material resources to make as
perfect a mummy as Egyptian ingenuity in
the whole of its experience was capable of
doing.

But the Egyptian tomb-robbers brought
to the attention of the official world many
mummies of the earlier part of the eighteenth
dynasty, as well as some of those of the
nineteenth and twentieth dynasties respectively
before and after the culmination of the technical
success in or about Tutankhamen's time which
revealed only too clearly certain faults that
it seemed desirable to remedy.

The wholesale plundering of the Royal
mummies in the twentieth dynasty, and the
knowledge acquired by the priests when
remedying the damage so inflicted, seem to
have been responsible for the rapid transfor-
mation of the methods in the twenty-first
dynasty.   For this experience afforded them
a unique opportunity of studying the results
and appreciating the defects of their predecessors' work.

That they profited by this experience is
evident from the changes they effected in their
technique after they had realized wherein the

methods employed during the twentieth dynasty failed to attain the desired aim. For their innovations were directed towards remedying the most obtrusive distortions found in the mummies of the nineteenth and twentieth dynasties. The sunken cheeks were filled out by means of packing them with linen or mud, artificial eyes were inserted, the nose, lips, and ears were protected from distortion by wax plates, and the cheeks were painted. Many other devices were introduced to convert the mummy from a shrunken caricature into a more life-like portrait.

Mummification reached its fullest and most successful development during the six centuries from 1500 B.C. to 940 B.C., which represents the period of the collection of royal mummies in the Cairo Museum. They reveal the ancient Egyptian practice of embalming in its highest perfection, and have provided most of the information we possess of the history of mummification.

I have called attention to the aims which the ancient Egyptians kept so persistently in view in constructing and furnishing the tombs of their kings. The pharaoh's body was embalmed to make sure of the continuation of his existence beyond the grave. The conviction

that this object was really attained when the
mummy was made and housed in an imperishable building induced them to furnish the tomb
lavishly and to provide an ample store of food
to sustain him and give him all the comforts
and luxuries to which he was accustomed when
he was living upon earth.   But, to make doubly
sure, they inscribed upon the walls of his tomb,

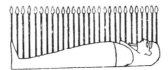

Fig. 9.—Drawing from Book of the Dead to illustrate
the Germinating Osiris, from Rosellini.

upon his sarcophagus and coffins, and on papyri
placed in the tombs, certain texts to make clear
his identification with Osiris, with the practical
object of ensuring that he should share the fate
of the god and attain the immortality which
the god had secured.   Moreover, other devices
were adopted to make the issue more certain.

Of the objects found in association with the
mummies of Egyptian kings of the eighteenth
dynasty to which definite cultural importance
was attached, none is more remarkable than
the so-called " germinating Osiris."   Several

examples of this singular symbol were found
in the tombs of Tutankhamen's predecessors,
as far back as Amenhotep II. (1420 B.C.), and
as it was observed in its fullest development in
the tomb of his successor, Horemheb(1315 B.C.),
it is more probable than not that Tutankhamen's
will also be similarly equipped.   It consists of
a shallow box about 5 ft. long, shaped so as
to represent the god Osiris, wearing a crown
and holding the crook and whip in his hands.
By means of wooden partitions the features of
the head, the necklace, the arms are represented.
This shallow box was filled with earth in which
barley was planted; when it germinated and
the sprouts had attained two or three inches in
height a closely-fitting lid was fastened on to
the box by wooden pegs.   The lid is slightly
sculptured en ronde bosse, and painted yellow.
The details of the body and the ornaments
are indicated in relief, the effect of which is
heightened by lines of black and red.

The King and Osiris

The symbolism expressed in this remarkable
procedure was in keeping with the motives
which were explained earlier in this chapter,
the identification of the dead king with Osiris
(who was himself a dead king), whose magical

powers as the bestower of renewed life and a continuation of existence after death was symbolized by the germinating barley.

But the procedure was richly charged with the deepest religious significance. I have already explained that the whole of the burial customs of the early Egyptians and the dramatic ritual which formed part of the tomb ceremonies were inspired by the desire to ensure the prolongation of existence. The body was made imperishable and protected by every means the relatives could devise : it was supplied with abundance of food and all the necessaries of life ; and, above all, the "germinating Osiris" was there to complete the process and perpetually to animate and prolong the existence of the corpse. If its potency was derived from the reproduction of the form of Osiris, an equally vital part of its supposed magical power was due to the fact that it consisted of barley in the act of producing new life.

As the earliest cereal that was cultivated and the staple diet of the earliest civilized people—and the chief factor in creating their civilization—barley came to occupy a peculiarly distinctive rôle in early belief. It was the staff of life and the material from which beer was

made, the drink which was regarded as
" divine," in the sense that life-giving qualities
were attributed to it, and to the ancient
Egyptian the essence of divinity was the
attainment of unlimited existence. But the
form assumed by a grain of barley (*i.e.* its
similarity to the organ of birth, the giver of
life) led to the assimilation of its life-sustaining
with definitely life-giving functions. It was
identified with the Great Mother as a life-
giver (in her forms as Hathor or Isis) ; and
the " corn mother" acquired the reputation
of being able to prolong existence in other
ways than providing food and drink. The
coffin texts of the Middle Kingdom (*circa*
2000 B.C.) translated by M. Lacau refer to the
identification of the deceased with Osiris and
barley, and in the Pyramid texts many
centuries earlier the dead king is represented
as making the following claim : " I am Osiris.
I live as the gods ; I live as ' Grain ' ; I grow as
' Grain.' I am barley." (Professor Breasted's
translation.) Just as the Nile (which was
personified as Osiris) conveyed new life to the
grains of barley by irrigating them, so the god
was supposed to be able to grant a new lease
of existence to the dead.

CHAPTER V

THE VALLEY OF THE TOMBS

It was about the year 1500 B.C. that the desolate and impressive ravine which is now known as the Valley of the Tombs of the Kings was chosen by King Thothmes I as the site for his tomb. His immediate predecessor Amenhotep I had observed the practice, which had prevailed since the temple was first invented, of building the tomb in association with it. For the temple was a development of the rooms provided at the tomb for the relations of the deceased to make offerings of food and drink to the dead for the essentially practical purpose of maintaining his existence. In these rooms also certain ceremonies were performed from time to time with the object of animating the dead man (or his portrait statue) so that he could enjoy the food and commune with his relations. But such functions were also part of the process of conveying "life" to him and so ensuring the maintenance of his existence.

In course of time as these ceremonies for

Fig. 10.—The end of the desolate Valley of the Tombs of the Kings at Thebes, the most impressive site in the whole of Egypt.

conveying sustenance and life to a dead king assumed a wider significance the chamber of

offering developed into a temple and a subtle
change occurred in the meaning attached to
the ritual. For instead of being regarded

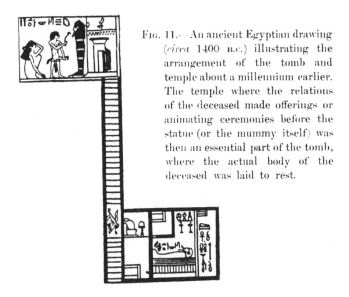

FIG. 11.—An ancient Egyptian drawing
(*circa* 1400 B.C.) illustrating the
arrangement of the tomb and
temple about a millennium earlier.
The temple where the relations
of the deceased made offerings or
animating ceremonies before the
statue (or the mummy itself) was
then an essential part of the tomb,
where the actual body of the
deceased was laid to rest.

merely as a physical device for conveying food
and the essence of life the ceremonies came to
be regarded more and more as acts of worship
of the dead king. When this happened the
close nexus between the temple and the tomb
was no longer so essential as it was in earlier
times when the ceremonial in the former was
intended to vitalize the corpse of the king (or

his substitute the portrait statue). But it was
not until the closing years of the sixteenth
century B.C. (Thothmes I is believed to have
died in 1501 B.C.) that the king began to
prepare a tomb for himself miles away from
his temple. This geographical separation of
the temple from the tomb had a far-reaching
influence upon the functions of the former,
and prepared the way for the modern conception of a house of worship, even though in
Europe the ancient conception of the close
association of a church and a churchyard (as
a burying place) was retained. The practice
inaugurated by Thothmes I of preparing royal
tombs in the famous Theban Valley lasted
from about 1500 B.C. until the end of the
twentieth dynasty, about 1090 B.C.

Amenhotep III, who was buried in 1375
B.C., broke away from the observances of his
four predecessors who were buried in the
Eastern Valley and made his tomb in the
Western Valley; and his famous son and
successor, Amenhotep IV, the heretic king
Akhenaton, made the more daring innovation
of preparing a tomb at his new capital, the
City of the Horizon of Aton, on the site of
the modern Tell el Amarna. It was a rock-
cut tomb in the mountains about seven

miles to the east of his new capital—which
Akhenaton built midway (p. 22) between
Thebes and Memphis, the ancient capitals of
Upper and Lower Egypt respectively. There
he seems to have been buried in the red granite
sarcophagus that is now broken into fragments; but his son-in-law Tutankhamen,
when he reverted to the orthodox religion of
Thebes, thought it proper to remove the
mummy of his father-in-law from the City of
the Horizon to the Theban necropolis and
made for it the resting place in the Valley of
the Tombs, which was discovered in 1907 by
Mr Arthur Weigall, who as Inspector of
Antiquities for Upper Egypt was supervising
the excavations endowed by the late Mr
Theodore M. Davis.

The fate of the mummy of Akhenaton's
successor Smenkhara is unknown: but Tutankhamen came after him, and Mr Howard
Carter's discovery has shown that he displayed
his return to strict orthodoxy by making his
tomb in the Eastern Valley among the wor-
shippers of Amen. For some reason which
has not been fully elucidated, his successor Ay
made his tomb in the Western Valley and so
was laid to rest alongside Amenhotep III,
whose Minister he seems to have been during

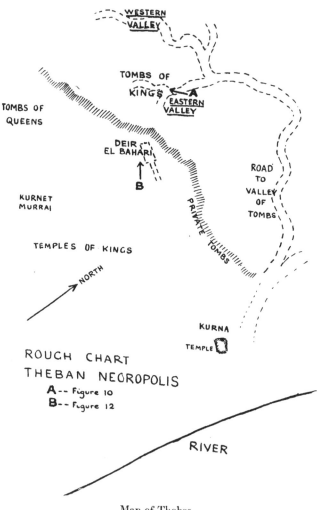

WESTERN
VALLEY

TOMBS OF
KINGS   A

TOMBS OF
QUEENS

EASTERN
VALLEY

DEIR
EL BAHARI

ROAD
TO
VALLEY
OF
TOMBS

B

KURNET
MURRAI

PRIVATE TOMBS

TEMPLES OF KINGS

NORTH

KURNA
TEMPLE

ROUGH CHART
THEBAN NECROPOLIS
    A -- Figure 10
    B -- Figure 12

RIVER

Map of Thebes.

his life.   He is supposed by some historians
to have been the father or the foster-father of
Nefertiti, the wife of Akhenaton.

Until the discovery of Tutankhamen's tomb
in the Eastern Valley last November it was
believed (by Sir Gaston Maspero and others)
that it would be found in the Western Valley.
Until then Ay's was the earliest royal tomb,
after that of Amenhotep III, to be discovered,
and as they were in the Western Valley, it
seemed probable that Ay's predecessor Tutankhamen had also been buried there.   But when
making the secondary tomb for Akhenaton in
the Eastern Valley he seems to have made
his own tomb there also, and so resumed the
old practice, which was observed by all his
successors for two and a half centuries with
the exception only of his successor Ay.

This wonderfully impressive gorge (Fig.
10, p. 66) is known to the modern Egyptians
as the *Bab* (or *Bibun*) *el Moluk*, the Gate (or
Gates) of the Kings.   It was known to
travellers ever since it was made into the royal
necropolis, and Greeks and Romans marvelled
at the wonderful tunnel-like tombs there, as
generations of tourists have done ever since.
Strabo mentions his having seen forty of these
tombs, but it is not clear from his account

whether he did not include those of the Western Valley and perhaps the Tombs of the Queens and others.

Modern research was inaugurated by the traveller Belzoni who opened the tomb of Seti I in 1819 and described the pictures on its walls (Fig. 20 is copied from his note-book) before they were damaged or destroyed. He brought to London the magnificent "alabaster" sarcophagus of this pharaoh, which is now in Sir John Soane's museum in Lincoln's Inn Fields.

The year 1881 will always be memorable for the earliest discovery of Royal mummies. Five years later, when the wrappings were removed from such pharaohs as Seti I and Rameses II, modern men had the novel experience of gazing upon the actual faces of these famous rulers of the remotely distant past, whose exploits had resounded through the civilized world for thirty centuries and more. On several occasions in former years the discovery of Royal mummies had been reported; but in every case further investigation failed to justify such claims, for they proved to be merely intrusive burials of unknown people belonging to times much later than the rifled tombs in which they were found. Examples of such mistakes in identification are the eighteenth dynasty mummy, now in the Cairo Museum, which was found in a pyramid at Sakkara, and at one time was supposed to be the son of King Pepi, of the sixth dynasty; and the skeleton (not a mummy) in the British Museum from the pyramid of Mykerinus, which has repeatedly been referred to as the bones, or even as the mummy, of that pharaoh.

The discoveries made in the famous cache at Deir el Bahari in 1881, and in the Valley of the Tombs of the Kings during the decade 1898-1908, revealed the only actual mummies of members of the royal family so far recovered, although the skeletons of much earlier members of the ruling house were found by M. de Morgan in the pyramids of Dashur nearly thirty years ago.

Long before the recovery of the actual bodies of these famous rulers the statues and bas-reliefs of some of them had familiarized us with their appearance; and inscriptions on their monuments and the ancient writings of the Egyptians and their neighbours had made us acquainted with certain of their exploits. The plundered tombs of some of the great kings of the eighteenth and nineteenth dyn-

F

Fig. 12.—An old photograph of the great cliffs behind Deir el Bahari, showing this temple as it was in 1881 before it was excavated. The royal mummies were hidden in a cleft in these cliffs.

asties have been known and visited by tourists
from the times of the Greek domination of
Egypt, and contemporary documents refer to
others.   Moreover, twenty years before the
mummies themselves were revealed, the dealers
in antiquities began to offer for sale a series of
papyri (most of which came to this country)
giving accounts of the desecration of the royal
Theban tombs.

Tomb-robbers' Confessions

In the late Lord Amherst's collection, which
was recently sold in London, there was a
judicial papyrus of the reign of Rameses IX
(about 1125 B.C.), reporting the trial of eight
"servants of the High Priest of Amen," who
were arraigned for plundering the tomb of
King Sebekemsaf of the thirteenth dynasty.
The written depositions of the prisoners set
before the pharaoh by the vizier, the lieutenant,
the reporter, and the mayor of Thebes were
translated by Professor Percy Newberry in
these terms: "We opened the coffins and
their wrappings, which were on them, and we
found the noble mummy of the king.   There
were two swords and many amulets and neck-
laces of gold on his neck : his head was covered
with gold.   We tore off the gold that we

found on the noble mummy of this god [*i.e.* the dead king who was identified with Osiris]. We found the royal wife also. We tore off all that we found from her mummy likewise, and we set fire to their wrappings. We took their furniture of gold, silver and copper vases, which we found with them." The prisoners who made this confession were found guilty, and sentenced " to be placed in the prison of the temple of Amen," to await " the punishment that our lord the pharaoh shall decide." There are several other famous papyri reporting trials of desecrators of the royal tombs. In the Abbott papyrus (in the British Museum) inspectors submit a report on the tombs that were said to have been plundered, but the only one that had actually been robbed was that referred to in the confession just quoted from the Amherst papyrus. The two Mayer papyri in the Liverpool Free Public Museums relate to plundering in the Valley of the Tombs of the Kings. One of these is of special interest at the present moment because it relates to the violation of the tomb of Rameses VI, which is immediately above that of Tutankhamen. The robbers were discovered as the result of quarrels among themselves about the division of the spoil. This

was one of the most disgraceful incidents
in the whole history of tomb-plundering.
The robbers, in their haste to get at the
gold and jewels upon the mummies, usually
chopped through the bandages, and mutilated
the mummy in the process. But when, in
1905, I removed the wrappings from the
mummy of Rameses VI (which in ancient
times had been removed to the tomb of
Amenhotep II, where it was discovered by
M. Loret in 1898), the body was found to be
hacked to pieces. This was no mere accidental
injury, but clearly intentional destruction of a
malicious nature. It makes one realize the
sort of vandalism Tutankhamen's tomb so
narrowly escaped.

Hiding the Mummies

The discovery of the royal mummies in
1881—and this applies with special force to
the remains of the famous pharaohs Seti I
and Rameses II—gave us the other side of
the story, for it revealed the measures taken
to protect the bodies of these kings from
further injury, and the persistence with which
the protectors of the tombs moved the
mummies from one place to another in their
endeavour to save them. The condition of

affairs revealed in the tomb of Tutankhamen brings proof of what has long been suspected, that the work of the plunderer began soon after the closing of the chambers. But during the twentieth and twenty-first dynasties, when there was a rapid weakening of the Administration, tomb-robbing assumed proportions it had never attained before. The record inscribed upon the coffins of Seti I and Rameses II throws a lurid light on the extent of this loss of control. For a century and a half their mummies were moved from one hiding-place to another in the attempt to secure their safety. The mummy of the great Rameses was moved to the tomb of his father, Seti I, whose body for some time remained in its own alabaster sarcophagus, which is now in Sir John Soane's Museum in Lincoln's Inn Fields. But in the reign of Siamon (976-958 B.C.) the two mummies were hidden in the tomb of a queen called Inhapi, and about ten years later were moved again, this time to a tomb that had been originally prepared for Amenhotep I at Deir el Bahari. Here they, together with more than thirty other royal mummies, remained undisturbed for more than twenty-eight centuries, until about fifty years ago they were rediscovered, and the successors of

the ancient tomb-robbers of Thebes once more
resumed the old process of depredation.   But
the late Sir Gaston Maspero had not studied
the papyri of the twentieth dynasty in vain,

FIG. 13.—The lid of the
coffin that contained
the rewrapped mum-
my of Amenhotep III,
to show how it was
labelled by the Priests
of the twentieth dyn-
asty and the record of
an inspection written
alongside it.

for he obtained a confession that is worthy of
being set beside those recorded in the Amherst
and Mayer papyri.

The story of the ill-treatment of the royal
mummies and of their repeated removal from
one hiding-place to another prepared us in
some measure for the discoveries that were

made when the shrouds and linen bandages
were removed. But in spite of this the investigation was full of surprises. Several of
the mummies after being hastily rewrapped
(in the twentieth or twenty-first dynasty)
were put into the wrong coffins. So that,
for example, when the mummy supposed to
be Rameses I (of the nineteenth dynasty)
was unwrapped, an old white-haired lady was
found embalmed in a way distinctive of the
early part of the eighteenth dynasty. And
again, when the mummy in the coffin of
Setnakht (the first king of the twentieth
dynasty) was examined, it was found to be
that of a woman embalmed in the manner
distinctive of the time of Setnakht's predecessor (Seti II, of the nineteenth dynasty);
and it is probable that she is Queen Tausret,
the wife in turn of the two kings, Siptah and
Seti II. Such discoveries reveal the need for
caution in claiming that the Valley of the
Tombs of the Kings has yielded up all its
hidden secrets. For there are many royal
mummies that we know to have been buried
there which have yet to be recovered.

If the examination of the royal mummies
reveals the thoroughness with which the
tombs have been rifled—not one of the series

has ever been found undisturbed—they also
give us some idea of the value of the jewellery
and amulets which excited the greed of the
robbers thirty centuries ago. The torn and
mutilated wrappings of the mummies often
bear the impressions of magnificent pectoral
ornaments, and of amulets on the forehead,
neck, or limbs; and the occasional finding of
fragments of these, made of gold, lapis lazuli,
or carnelian, gives us some idea of the value
and beauty of this extravagant equipment of
the dead. But I have known only one
instance of an object of any considerable
intrinsic value escaping the diligent searching
of these experienced robbers. During the
examination (in 1909) of the badly plundered
mummy of Queen Hontaui I found a large and
beautifully embossed plate of pure gold, unique
in size and in the elaboration of its design.

From these considerations we can safely
predict that if, as seems now to be certain,
the unplundered mummy is found in the
tomb of Tutankhamen jewellery of great
value and beauty of design will probably be
found on it. The superb workmanship displayed in making these ornaments and amulets
is known to us from the discoveries made by
M. de Morgan in the Pyramids at Dashur in

1893. These gold pectoral ornaments inlaid with precious stones were wrought with an amazing perfection of technical skill many centuries before the time of Tutankhamen; but the jewellery of the eighteenth and nineteenth dynasties now exhibited in many museums (especially the Cairo Museum and the Louvre) reveals that the skill in making such works of art had not been lost. The quality of the workmanship revealed in the objects found in the first chamber of Tutankhamen's tomb should prepare us for the discovery on the mummy of ornaments even surpassing those of Rameses II in the Louvre (see Maspero, *Egyptian Art*).

But the chief interest in the discovery should be in the mummy itself, for the welfare of which all the elaborate arrangements were made. It is not merely because the mummies enable us to form some idea of the physical features of the kings and queens, and by appealing to our common humanity give their personalities a reality they would not otherwise possess; nor is it because they often reveal evidence of age and infirmities; their chief interest is the light they throw on the history of the period and upon the development of the art of embalming.

Perhaps I can best make plain what is
meant by this statement if I refer to specific
illustrations of the former kind of contribution
the study of mummies makes to the fuller
understanding of history.

When in 1907 the bones were found that
had once formed part of the mummy wrongly
assumed to be the famous Queen Tiy, I discovered that they were the remains of a
young man's skeleton, for which, if it had
been normal, it was difficult to admit an age
of more than twenty-six years, if indeed as
much. Now the archæological evidence seems
to leave no loophole of escape from the con-
clusion that these bones are actually the
skeleton of King Akhenaton; but, on the
other hand, the historical evidence seems to
demand an age of at least thirty years (or,
according to a recent memoir by Professor
Kurt Sethe, thirty-six years) for the famous
heretic pharaoh. This apparent conflict between
the two classes of evidence has stimulated an
intensive study of the historical data and of
the medical history of Akhenaton himself;
and the final outcome of the investigations
is likely to provide a most illuminating revelation of the inner meaning of perhaps the
most human and dramatic incident that has

come to us from ancient times. The peculiar
features of Akhenaton's head and face, the
grotesque form assumed by his legs and body,
no less than the eccentricities of his behaviour,
and his pathetic failure as a statesman, will
probably be shown to be due to his being
the subject of a rare disorder, only recently
recognized by physicians, who have given it
the cumbrous name Dystocia adiposo-genitalis.
One of the effects of this condition is to
delay the process of the consolidation of
the bones. Studying the history of modern
instances of this affection the possibility
suggests itself that Akhenaton might well
have attained the age of thirty or even
thirty-six years, although his bones are in a
condition which in the normal individual is
appropriate to the years twenty-two to twenty-
six. It is tempting to speculate on the vast
influence on the history of the world, not
merely the political fate of Egypt and Syria
in the fourteenth century B.C., but the religious
conceptions of Palestine and the whole world
for all time, for which the illness of this pacifist
poet may have been largely responsible.

There is still a vast amount of information
to be got from the study of the royal
mummies in the light of modern knowledge,

and by the use of technical methods that are
now for the first time available: and one of
the hopes raised by the new discoveries is
that it may be possible to set an example
of how such work ought to be carried out,
so as to extract from the remains of these
ancient pharaohs all the information they can
give us.

The importance of the study of the technique
of mummification as a means of revealing the
past history of civilization (by affording evidence of the diffusion of culture which was
the chief factor in the process of cultural
development) is too large a subject to embark
on here.   I mention it only because most of
the exact information we have of the history
of embalming has been derived from the royal
mummies themselves.

In my pamphlet *The Migrations of Early
Culture* (1915) I made use of the evidence
afforded by the geographical distribution of
the practice of mummification to demonstrate
the diffusion to the ends of the earth in
ancient times of elements of culture that were
derived directly or indirectly from Egypt.

In the *Revue Neurologique* for 1920 two
French physicians, Drs M. Ameline and
P. Quercy, published a very curious memoir

with the title " Le Pharaon Aménophis IV, sa mentalité. Fut-il atteint de Lipodystrophie Progressive ? " I have used the adjective curious with reference to their work, because they have put forward a carefully reasoned statement in support of the diagnosis they suggest, but do not seem to have made any attempt to make themselves acquainted with the evidence provided by the remains of the pharaoh. When it is recalled that in 1912 I gave a detailed account (*The Royal Mummies*, Catalogue Générale du Musée du Caire) of the broken bones which were all that was left of the mummy of the pharaoh (no trace of the mummy of his mother, Queen Tiy, has been found), it is surprising to find in a scientific journal the following statements, written ten years after the appearance of my official report was published :—" on a retrouvé récemment (1905), à Thèbes même, les *momies* du pharaon *et de sa mère Tii*," and, referring to the remains of Akhenaton, *i.e.* the broken fragments of the skeleton, " La momie, recouverte de feuilles d'or délicatement repoussé et d'un réseau d'or avec pierres et verres colorés, *est également exceptionnellement belle, mais ces ornements empêchent naturellement d'examiner le corps du pharaon aux rayons X et, a fortiori, d'en practiquer l'autopsie ?"* (*op. cit.*, p. 451.   All the italics are mine).

I have quoted these purely imaginary statements to emphasize the fact that the distin-

Fig. 14.—An inscribed stone from Tell el Amarna, showing Akhenaton, his queen Nefertiti, and their daughters, all represented by the sculptor as suffering from the same dystocia as Akhenaton himself.

guished physicians who made them were totally ignorant of the conditions revealed in the skull, and based their diagnosis wholly upon the pictures of Akhenaton and the history of his achievements. They describe the condition of progressive lipodystrophy as an affection characterized on the one hand by a progressive and complete disappearance of the subcutaneous fat of the upper part of the body; and, on the other, by a marked increase of the adipose tissue below the loins. The first example of this strange affection was described by Barraquer in 1907, but it is exceedingly rare in adult men. In fact the authors remark that "it would indeed be curious if a pharaoh, dead for thirty-five centuries, should provide a second case (after Gertsmann's) of the occurrence of this condition in an adult man."

It is unfortunate that these physicians neglected to study the report which I wrote for the General Catalogue of the Cairo Museum, published in the volume *The Royal Mummies* in 1912. For they would then have realized that the slight hydrocephalus, the indication of an early overgrowth of the jaw such as occurs in acromegaly, and then the gradual assumption of a feminine contour of figure, with a delayed union of the epiphyses, suggest the possibility that Akhenaton may have been the subject of Dystocia adiposo-genitalis.

FIG. 15.—A painted wooden portrait bust of Nefertiti, wife of
Akhenaton.

The form of the head in Akhenaton, his daughters and some of the members of his family, more than half a century before his

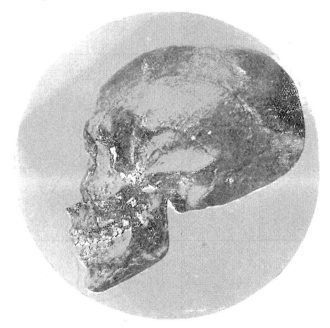

Fig. 16.—The skull of Akhenaton seen from the left side.

time, raises a problem of great difficulty and complexity.

There is no doubt that the slight malformation of Akhenaton's head was due to pathological causes. It is equally certain that the gross distortion of the heads of his daughters,

represented in the statues from Tell el Amarna
which are now in Berlin, are the result of
artificial deformation such as was and still is
practised upon young children in Asia Minor
and Northern Syria, with the royal family of
which Akhenaton's family was linked by close
ties.   But in addition the mummy of a boy
in the tomb of Amenhotep II, which was
certainly embalmed in the reign of that
pharaoh and is probably the body of his
son, has a skull which is exceptionally broad
and flat, and when viewed from the front
presents an appearance curiously similar to
the portrait statues of Akhenaton's daughters.
The full significance of these peculiarities
cannot be interpreted until the royal mummies
now in the Cairo Museum are submitted to a
thorough re-examination.

CHAPTER VI

THE STORY OF THE FLOOD

JUST half a century ago[1] the proprietors of
The Daily Telegraph arranged with the
Trustees of the British Museum to send Mr
George Smith to Mesopotamia to search in
the ruins of the library of Ashur-bani-pal at
Nineveh for missing fragments of inscribed
tablets to fill the gaps in the *Chaldean Account
of the Deluge.* The announcement of the
discovery (in December 1872) aroused an
intense and world-wide interest, and *The
Daily Telegraph* provided the funds for the
new expedition. Although this version of the
Story of the Flood was discovered in an
Assyrian library no older than the seventh
century B.C., Mr George Smith predicted that
the future would reveal it to be the survival
of a more ancient version that had also indirectly been the inspiration of that recorded
in the Book of Genesis. The recent discovery
of the Sumerian prototype of this story, which

---

[1] This was written in January 1923.

was put into writing more than twenty centuries before the record in Ashur-bani-pal's library, is a remarkable confirmation of George Smith's prediction.

It will come as a surprise to most people to learn that the Valley of the Tombs in Egypt has provided the information which is destined in time to afford the explanation of the early history of the Story of the Flood, before it began to exert a strange fascination upon the minds of men that led to its diffusion throughout the world.

Inscribed upon the walls of the tomb of Seti I in the Theban necropolis—less than seventy years after the burial of Tutankhamen —is the remarkable story of the Destruction of Mankind. In spite of the fact that it was inscribed in this tomb as recently—in comparison with the Sumerian story—as 1300 B.C., the strange confusion of archaic references which has made it so unintelligible to most modern scholars reveals the fact that its origin must be referred back to the fourth millennium. Although in the narrative found in Seti's tomb the destruction is not brought about by the Flood, it is clear that the Egyptian and the Mesopotamian stories have a common origin and a common motive. For the essential incident in the latter is not the Flood, but the Destruction of Mankind which it brought to pass.

If it be asked why this venerable story should be inscribed in the tomb of an Egyptian pharaoh, the answer is that its aim was to secure for the dead king those boons the attainment of which was the central motive of the tale. It records how old age began to affect the king, upon whose strength and virility the welfare of the whole community depended (see Chapter IV), and he became very sorely troubled when his subjects began to murmur about the failure of his powers, because in olden days the only way of safeguarding the prosperity of the kingdom, which was supposed to be wholly dependent upon the strength of its ruler, was to slay him when he began to fail and put in his place one whose vigour was at its prime.

The essence of the story, which made it potent as a charm to secure the continued existence of the king (and it was for this reason that it was inscribed upon the walls of the king's tomb) was that it describes how the ageing king circumvented fate (and the conventions of archaic society) by rejuvenating himself. The elixir of life was the blood of

his slaughtered subjects; and the crime that
was charged against them—the impiety and
disloyalty, the original sin — was that they
were murmuring among themselves about the
king's failing health. But when they had
been slaughtered and the king had attained a
renewal of his youth, he was overcome by the
boredom of too prolonged an existence upon
earth. So he mounted upon the back of the
Celestial Cow and thus reached heaven and
attained immortality.

This remarkable story, which was intended
as a magical device for securing the same fate
for the pharaoh of the fourteenth century B.C.
as his remote prototype is said to have attained,
also contains the germs of most of the myth-
ology that has lasted longest and spread most
widely in the early history of civilization.
Although, so far as we are aware, this story is
not found in Tutankhamen's tomb, there is no
doubt that it was current at his time, because
it was inscribed upon the walls of one of his
successor's tombs little more than half a century
later, and the narrative is obviously very old,
being packed with archaic allusions and forms
of expression. I have referred to it here
because the symbolism expressed in some of
the funerary furniture in Tutankhamen's tomb

is explained by this mythical story recorded
in those of Seti I and Rameses III. The
question of interpretation I have discussed in
another chapter, dealing with the funerary
couches, and I have mentioned the Destruction
of Mankind to call attention to the dominant
motive—the Giving of Life and the Attainment of Immortality—which inspires every
feature of the funerary ritual with tiresome
persistence. For in the myth mankind was
destroyed to provide the elixir of life for the
king so that he might attain to the immortality,
which was the distinctive prerogative of a god.
The blood of the slaughtered saints was the
elixir by which the mortal dweller on earth
put on the immortality of a celestial being.
The motive assigned in the story for destroying
mankind was their sinfulness or disloyalty,
which was more exactly defined by accusing
them of spreading rumours of the king's increasing age and weakness, a form of report
to which the ruler was peculiarly sensitive,
because the admission that his strength and
virility were failing was tantamount to a
capital sentence. In the remotely distant age,
from which the germs of this story came down
to the time of Seti I, the ageing king had to
be killed to make way for a more youthful

and vigorous ruler.   Hence one cannot marvel at the king's sensitiveness when his people murmured about his failing powers.

I have already referred to the fact that this accusation of disloyalty was the earliest version of what theologians call " original sin," and the story itself the prototype of that which under a modified form appears in the Book of Genesis. The primitive account of the slaying of mankind became confused with the inundation of the Nile, and the blood of the slaughtered human race and the blood-red inundation of the river became identified the one with the other. Though originally both events were regarded as beneficent and identical in their results, that is renewing the king's strength and the country's prosperity, when the story spread abroad to foreign countries a certain element of confusion crept into the narrative, and the destruction of mankind was attributed to the Flood.   But it found a place in religious literature, not because it exemplified the wrath of the gods against sinful man, but because it explained how the king rejuvenated himself and attained the status of a god.   The evidence provided by these Egyptian tombs gives us an insight into the motives underlying the religious beliefs of every people who came into relationship, directly or indirectly, with the arbitrary system of explaining the means of attaining immortality devised by the ancient priesthood of Egypt. It illustrates one of the ways in which these investigations in Egypt can illuminate ancient Jewish literature.

One of the peculiarities of Egyptian customs and beliefs is due to the fact that what the concrete-minded Egyptian naïvely did and said is to be interpreted in the literal and obvious sense that he attached to these acts. Among no other people can we similarly detect all the stages in the logical development of the practices and beliefs of civilization—and not only are the various stages preserved in Egypt, but in so crudely childlike a guise that he who overcomes the impulse to seek for some recondite or cryptic meaning in things which are really simple can read their plain story as their inventors intended it.

It is this fundamental fact that gives the study of Egyptian customs and beliefs its tremendous importance. The essential elements of civilization were originally invented by the Egyptians, who gave them simpler and more obvious expression than other peoples, who borrowed them ready - made without acquiring the connecting stages in their development or the naïve explanation of their meaning.

I have introduced this subject for consideration as an introduction to the study of the funerary equipment of Tutankhamen's tomb, to which the next chapter will be devoted.

CHAPTER VII

It is not my intention to attempt to discuss the equipment of Tutankhamen's tomb. Readers of the daily papers and the illustrated weeklies will already be aware of the vast quantity of furniture and of the fact that even those who were already familiar with the superb design and workmanship displayed in the objects from such tombs as those of Thothmes IV, Yuaa and Tuaa, and Akhenaton were amazed at the new revelation of Egyptian craftsmanship revealed in scores of the things found in Tutankhamen's tomb, the throne, a superb work of art, the no less wonderful chariots, chairs, couches, statues, sandals, textiles and jewellery, and above all the impressive canopy or shrine. Archæologists familiar with all the marvels of Egyptian art, now treasured in the museums scattered throughout the world, have exhausted their vocabularies of wonder and admiration in attempting to depict the splendours of Tutan-

khamen's tomb. The outstanding feature of
the discovery is, in fact, the recovery of so
vast a collection of superb works of art and
the new revelation it affords of the dazzling brilliance of Egyptian civilization thirty
centuries ago.

But in this book I am concerned more
especially with the cultural significance of the
funerary equipment.

In the first place the objects found in the
tomb belong to two distinct categories, those
which were used by the deceased when alive,
and others specially made for funerary pur-
poses. This distinction seems to be brought
out most clearly in the comparison of the
chariots in the vestibule and in the burial
chamber respectively.

I do not propose to enter into any further
discussion of the contents of the wonderful
shrine or canopy which is to be investigated
next winter, nor to attempt to anticipate the
result of the examination of the so-called
" canopic " chest, which is said to be a unique
example of the sculptor's art. The experience
gained in investigating the contents of such
chests in other tombs gives one confidence in
assuming that the heart of Tutankhamen will
not be found in it, as so many writers imagine,

but that its four compartments will contain
respectively the liver, lungs, stomach and
intestines of Tutankhamen, his "heart and
reins" being left in his body.

From the cultural point of view the most
interesting articles of furniture found in
Tutankhamen's tomb are the three lofty
couches fashioned in grotesque shapes to
represent conventionalized animals, cow, lion,
and hippopotamus respectively.   Although
such couches are thoroughly Egyptian in
design and are familiar in pictures from Egypt
and the Soudan, they have never been seen
before.   They are worth discussing in some
detail, because they express the concreteness
and naïvety of Egyptian belief mentioned in
the last chapter in a way that brings home to
us the essential distinction of the religion of
the ancient dwellers in the Nile Valley.

The problem of getting to heaven after death
was approached by the Egyptian theologian
as though it were essentially a physical pro-
position.   How was the dweller upon earth to
reach the world in the sky?   What vehicle
could he employ to reach the celestial realms?
Speaking recently of Christian Englishmen in
the twentieth century, Dean Inge is reported
to have said that "a topographical heaven, so

impossible scientifically, was so difficult to dispense with as an aid to the imagination." But to the ancient Egyptian belief in such a topographical heaven was a cardinal article of faith, and the geography of the Elysian fields and the details of the path leading to it were mapped out with all the meticulous precision of a modern guide-book. The dead man was often provided with a chart to find his way along the path that teemed with difficulties and dangers.

But although there were scores of different devices for securing a safe transit to the celestial regions, there was one vehicle which from the very beginning of Egyptian history enjoyed a special reputation as the appropriate means of protecting the dead and conferring life and immortality upon him by conveying him to the other world. The Celestial Cow Hathor not only conferred life upon mortals by giving them birth: she also sustained them throughout life by giving them the divine milk, and at death she conveyed them to the sky.

In the famous inscription upon the walls of the tomb of Seti I, to certain passages of which I referred in the last chapter, there is a remarkable story of the function of the Divine Cow Hathor or Nut as a means of raising the dead king to the sky to reach the home of the gods. After being rejuvenated by the goddess the king became oppressed with the boredom of life upon earth amongst his tiresome subjects, who had shown their disloyalty to him by referring to his old age and failing powers. So he decided to leave the earth and proceed to the sky. Hence he mounted upon the back of the cow and got to heaven, where he assumed his godhead by becoming identified with the sun.

This function of the cow in acting as a vehicle to convey the mummy to its celestial home is one which was repeatedly depicted in the ancient Egyptian monuments. But the cow's solicitude for the welfare of the dead was frequently shown in other ways. A favourite *motif* for the Egyptian sculptor was the representation of the Divine Cow, Hathor, protecting the dead king or permitting him to obtain an elixir of life by drinking milk from her udder. In his book *Egyptian Art* (1913) the late Sir Gaston Maspero devotes to this subject a whole chapter (XI) illustrated with six beautiful photographic plates of such cow-statues ranging from the time of Amenhotep II (1440 B.C.) to more than a thousand years later. But we know that the protective

function of the Cow Hathor was portrayed in
other ways as early as the time of the Pyramid-
builders (for example, the beautiful slate
statuettes found by Professor Reisner in the
Pyramid Temple of Mykerinus of the fourth

Fig. 17.—Cow carrying a dead man to heaven.

dynasty, about 2800 B.C.), and the still earlier
representation of her upon the slate palette
of King Narmer of the first dynasty, about
3400 B.C. For several reasons this palette is
a historical document of unique importance.
Engraved upon it is the earliest example of

writing that has come down from antiquity: but it is of interest in connexion with the discussion in this chapter. For at the upper corners of the palette the cow-headed Hathor is depicted and as a further protection the

Fig. 18. Narmer's belt with four Hathor cows' heads, *circa* 3400 B.C.

king wears upon his belt four cows' heads (Fig. 18) in place of the cowrie amulets of more primitive peoples.

The Celestial Cow, Hathor, was a divinity of the dead, for she was the Giver of Life who was supposed to be able to prolong existence beyond the grave, and as she was also identi-

fied with the sky she became the appropriate
vehicle to convey the dead to the celestial
regions where the sun-god dwelt.

The most bizarre objects found in the
vestibule of Tutankhamen's tomb are the
three ceremonial couches, one representing the
Celestial Cow, Hathor, the second the same
goddess in her lioness form, or more probably
her son and representative Horus in the form
of a lion, and the third Tauert, the hippopotamus goddess, who was the divine midwife.

In the numerous accounts of these remarkable monstrosities that have appeared, I have
not seen any attempt to explain their significance. Although such grotesque examples
of mortuary furniture have never been seen
before, the bas-reliefs upon the walls of tombs
in Egypt and Ethiopia, and the pictures illustrating the Book of the Dead inscribed on
papyri, have made us familiar with them.
Moreover, the chapters of the Book of the
Dead relating to " the raising of the funeral
bed " leave no doubt as to the ritual significance of these couches.

The sides of the Hathor couch are grotesque
models of the Divine Cow, the earliest of the
Great Mothers who were believed to have
bestowed life and prosperity on mankind. It

may seem strange that the artists of Tutankhamen's time should have perpetrated such a
monstrosity as this Hathor couch. When
religious motives impelled the designers to
fashion a piece of furniture in imitation of so
uncouchlike a creature as a cow, the artist was
set a task which was almost impossible of
realization unless he sacrificed his artistic
ideals. There can be no doubt that in this
case he escaped the dilemma by repressing
his æsthetic feelings and abandoning himself
whole-heartedly to the task of devising a model
which was almost wholly religious in conception.

To understand why the cow, of all creatures,
should have been selected for this purpose, we
must remember the relentless logic and per-
sistency that inspired all the preparations of
the tomb and its furniture. The mummification of the body and the elaborate arrangements for protecting it and ministering to its
wants were due to the belief that the continu-
ance of the deceased's existence had been
secured by these preparations. But to make
doubly certain, no device that would contribute
to the attainment of this aim was neglected.
Inscriptions were made on the walls of the
tomb, on the sarcophagus and coffins, and on

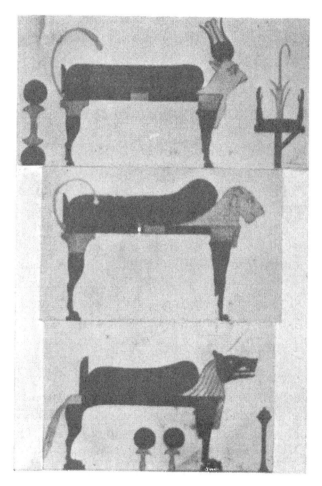

Fig. 19.—Pictures of three couches represented on the walls of
the tomb of Seti I, from Belzoni's sketches.

papyri to ensure the identification of the deceased king with Osiris, so that he might be made to share the god's fate. A figure of Osiris was made, as I have explained elsewhere (p. 61), out of the sacred barley, every grain of which was regarded as a model of the life-giving Great Mother, and as such a supply of vital essence to maintain the deceased's existence. From time to time dramatic ceremonies were held at the tomb (or in the temple associated with it in far-off Thebes) to reanimate the dead and help him to persist.

For, once the ancient Egyptians had persuaded themselves that they could work out their own salvation, and that the kingdom of heaven could be attained by certain physical and magical procedures, they spared no pains to pursue this train of thought and action with tiresome persistence to the most surprising ends.

The Great Mother was originally nothing more than the personification of an amulet, like a cowrie shell or a grain of barley, that was supposed to be able to exert the essentially maternal function of life-giving. Then, when cattle were domesticated and mankind discovered for the first time that cow's milk could be used for feeding human children, people were profoundly impressed with this revelation of the cow's kinship with the human family. They regarded her as the foster-mother, and then as the actual mother of mankind, and identified her with the Great Mother Hathor, whose earliest form was (even sixty centuries ago) that of a Divine Cow. But if the Great Mother was at one and the same time a cowrie, a grain of barley, and a cow, she was also identified with the moon, which in a very special sense was supposed to control the life-giving powers of womenkind.

Hence the belief developed that if the Great Giver of Life and Immortality was both a cow and the moon, she was the appropriate vehicle to convey the dead king to the celestial realms in the sky. And so, as the nursery rhyme puts it, "the cow jumped over the moon." That the cow represented in the couch is a symbol of the sky is shown by the stars on the under surface of the body. The height of the couches also was an additional indication of their identification with the sky. In all periods of Egyptian history painters and writers were fond of depicting this episode of the conveyance of the dead king to heaven on the cow's back. This incident is shown and explained in the inscriptions on the walls of Seti I's tomb, to which I have already re-

ferred (p. 95).   But in later times it became
common to represent the Divine Cow (or its
lioness surrogate) conveying the dead man or
his actual mummy to the sky, and in pictures
of funerals to find the mummy borne on just
such couches as have actually been found in
the tomb of Tutankhamen.   The object of the
cow-shaped couch was to ensure by magical
means this translation of the deceased to
heaven.   The story of the Destruction of
Mankind gives the Egyptian's own interpretation of the incident.   The influence of this
Egyptian conception of animal " vehicles " for
gods spread far and wide throughout the
world in ancient times, for if such a creature
could convey the dead king to the celestial
regions and confer upon him the means of
attaining immortality, which was the distinctive attribute of divinity, such an animal
vehicle was an appropriate symbol and pictorial
determinative of a god.   The identification of
the Great Mother with the cow was the
beginning of the social system known as
totemism.

The explanation of the lioness form of the
Great Mother is also given in the inscription
in Seti I's tomb.   When the goddess was
called upon to rejuvenate the ageing king, the

only elixir of life known in her pharmacopœia
was human blood. Hence, she was driven to
the necessity of slaying a human being, and
her murderous action was compared to that of
a man-slaying lioness, with which she was
identified. But as the lioness was a par-
ticularly appropriate form to symbolize the
Great Mother's ability to protect the mummy
from the perils that lurked in the pathway to
the other world, it became an even more
favourite form of the funerary vehicle than
the gentle cow. At any rate, in the pictures
of funerary couches the lioness form is much
commoner than the cow-form. The same
grotesque form of the lion has survived in
modern heraldry.

But other ideas found expression in the lion-
symbolism. For example, on some of the
beautiful pieces of furniture found in Tutankhamen's tomb the king himself is represented
as a human-headed lion trampling on his foes,
and many of his predecessors before him,
Thothmes IV for example, were similarly
represented. Even as far back as the time
of the Pyramids was not Mykerinus (2800 B.C.)
represented as a human-headed lion in the
gigantic Sphinx at the Giza Pyramids?

This representation of the king as a lion,

which typifies his identification with Horus, is
inspired by another chain of ideas.   Although
at the time of Tutankhamen, and in fact
throughout the whole history of Egypt in
dynastic times the sun-god was dominant
in Egypt and Horus himself was a sun-god,
the rôle that he took as the guardian of the
dead was inspired by the more ancient Osirian
faith.   It was the living king Horus who was
responsible for tending the dead king Osiris;
and it was believed that the continued existence
of the god (the dead king Osiris) was wholly
dependent upon the services rendered by Horus.
Thus it was Horus who performed the divine
function of conferring immortality upon Osiris,
and also upon the dead king Tutankhamen,
who was identified with Osiris.   Presumably
the act of being borne upon the lion-couch
was symbolically equivalent to being put into
the care of Horus, not the Horus represented
upon the furniture in the tomb, the lion-
avatar of Tutankhamen who tramples his
enemies under foot, but the son of Osiris,
who holds out the promise of conferring upon
the dead king the boons that he is credited
with having given to Osiris—eternal life and
protection.   The confusion between these two
aspects of Horus is brought out very clearly

in a very interesting picture recently discovered by Professor George A. Reisner (and reproduced in *The Illustrated London News*, 10th February 1923, p. 204), engraven upon a monument in the Soudan several centuries later than the time of Tutankhamen. The lion-couch is represented supporting the mummy of King Ergamenes, whose head is portrayed in the form of the falcon of Horus. Above the mummy is the star-spangled sky, below which is seen the sun's disc emitting five streams of life-giving emanations to the dead king. In the Book of the Dead Chapter LXXVIII is called that " whereby one assumeth the form of the Sacred Falcon " and the deceased is represented as saying " I display myself as the Sacred Falcon whom Horus hath invested with his soul for taking possession of his inheritance from Osiris " (Renouf). The possibility suggests itself whether the lion - couch was intended to symbolize, as the cow-couch unquestionably was, the transference of the dead king to the sky to be united with the sun and identified with the solar deity Re. If so, perhaps the five streams of V-shaped emanations pointing to the disc were meant to represent the sun drawing the mummy, the dead Horus, to the sky.

In his monograph of the *Tomb of Amenemhēt* Dr Alan Gardiner reproduces a text (Plate **XXX A**) including a pictorial arrangement of hieroglyphs in the form of stars above the mummy borne on the lion-couch, which he translates as a statement that the dead man "wishes to be placed among the stars in the firmament" (p. 119).

The same design occurs in the pictures illustrating the Book of the Dead. The funerary couch is usually represented in the lion-form, the cow- and hippopotamus-varieties being much less frequently adopted.

In the pictures of funerals it is not uncommon to see the mummy borne upon a lion-shaped couch placed within the funerary canopy or shrine (as in the first of the pictures from the Book of the Dead, Fig. 20). Good examples are given by Dr Alan Gardiner and Mrs de Garis Davies in *The Tomb of Amenemhēt* (1915), Plates **XII** and **XXIV**, of the reign of Thothmes III, a century before Tutankhamen. No doubt this is due partly to the significance attached to the conception of Horus as the guardian of Osiris, but also possibly to the idea that Horus fought the enemies of Re and was the best protector of the deified dead.

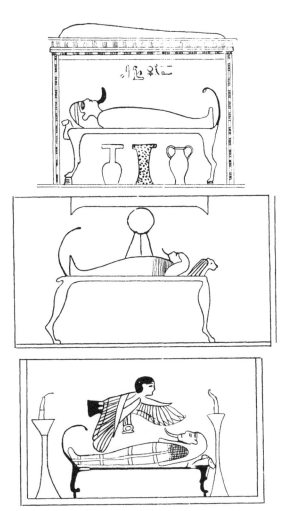

Fig. 20.—Three vignettes from different papyri of the Book of the Dead, representing the lion-couch bearing the mummy within its canopy, a mummy lying on its funerary couch with three solar emanations coming down from the sky, and a third where the bird-soul is bringing to the mummy the symbol of eternity.

But underlying the whole of the lion symbolism are two fundamental ideas which gave meaning to it. In the very ancient story of the Destruction of Mankind, which in a relatively modern and much distorted form was inscribed upon the walls of the tombs of several of Tutankhamen's successors, the goddess Hathor (the Divine Cow) is reported to have made a human sacrifice in order to obtain the blood wherewith to rejuvenate the senile king (in the story Re, the king upon earth who had not yet been elevated on the cow's back to the sky to become the sun-god). Hence she acquired the reputation as a slayer of men and was identified with a lioness, and called Sekhmet, the Destroyer. Thus the lioness and the cow were both forms assumed by the Great Mother Hathor. But in the development of the myth of the Destruction of Mankind the god Horus takes the place of his mother Hathor, and the bull and the lion take the place formerly occupied by the cow and the lioness. In the case of the funerary couches the Cow of Hathor is found alongside the lion of Horus, but occasionally one finds in late tombs the mummy represented as being conveyed to the celestial realms by a bull instead of the more usual cow. A good example of this is to be seen in the Museum of the Society of Antiquaries in Edinburgh.

The third couch is modelled in the form of a grotesque caricature of a hippopotamus, Taurt, another representative of the Great Mother Hathor. But her special duty was to act as a midwife at the births of gods and kings. In pictures she is often associated with the Hathor Cow at the door of the tomb in the Mountain of the West; and presumably her function was to preside at the rebirth of the dead king by which a new lease of life beyond the grave was conferred upon him.

If it seems far-fetched to regard the hippopotamus couch as symbolizing rebirth, it should not be overlooked that in the so-called " Birth Terrace " of the temple at Deir el Bahari[1] lion-headed couches are represented in the birth scene of Queen Hatshepsut. As I have pointed out already all three animals, cow, lioness, and female hippopotamus, represent primarily different forms of the same goddess Hathor.

The Egyptian custom of making these grotesque animal-shaped couches to symbolize

[1] See Egypt Exploration Fund publication. *Deir el Bahari*. II, Plate LI.

the transference of the dead to the celestial
regions and the conferring of immortality and
deification upon them exerted far-reaching and
manifold effects as it was diffused abroad among
other peoples.   I shall mention three examples

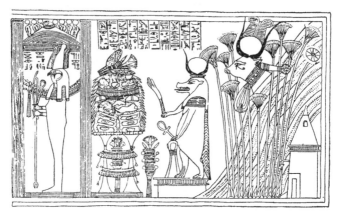

Fig. 21.—Scene from The Book of the Dead (Papyrus of Ani) in
which the three givers of divinity are seen, the cow at the
entrance to the tomb, the hippopotamus with her, and
Horus on guard.

of these diverse influences.   The belief implied
in such symbolism that a king borne by such
an animal vehicle was transformed into a god
led to the use of such designs in the repre-
sentations of gods.   Hence it became common
in Syria and Mesopotamia, in Greece and India,
and far away in outlying parts of the world

where the influence of these civilizations
played some part, directly or indirectly, to
find gods and goddesses represented on animal
vehicles, such as the bull or cow, the lion or

FIG. 22.—The goddess Astarte borne on her lioness, symbolizing
the attainment of immortality, which was the distinctive
attribute of a deity.

lioness, or some fantastic composite monster,
dragon or makara. The whole conception of
animal vehicles, which plays such a large part
in the religious symbolism of India, Eastern
Asia and Central America, is a purely Egyptian
fancy that finds such grotesque expression in
Tutankhamen's funerary couches, no less than

I

in the borrowed symbolism that was spread abroad from Egypt to Asia and America.

Another expression of the essential meaning of these couches was the belief that the placing of the corpse or mummy on a raised stage was magically efficacious in transferring the deceased to the sky world. The use of such raised platforms is practised over a very wide geographical area, and for the reasons given in my pamphlet *The Migrations of Early Culture* (1915). There can be no doubt that it gives expression to the same belief as the lofty and uncouth funerary beds in Tutankhamen's tomb have forced upon our attention.

Another wave of diffusion of culture is represented in the adoption by European furniture-makers of the Egyptian method of designing legs for chairs, beds and couches. In Egypt itself such a practice can be traced back to the first dynasty 3400 or more B.C. But the lion paws were adopted in Europe as a design for legs of chairs, etc. almost as soon as the Egyptian craft of carpentering and joinery was introduced. Long after the Queen Anne period Chippendale introduced the Chinese variant, the dragon's feet grasping the moon-pearl symbol. But as I explained in *The Evolution of the Dragon* (1919) the dragon is really a blending of Horus's falcon (eagle) and lion into one composite beast.

Thus the study of these couches has revealed the development in Egypt of a very peculiar but distinctive series of symbolic expressions, each of which is so arbitrary and unexpected that one is able to recognize it and refer it to its true source, in whatever part of the world and at whatever historical period it manifests itself.   Hence we are able to use the evidence provided by these three distinct aspects of one essential idea to demonstrate different waves of cultural diffusion which spread from Egypt throughout the world both in ancient and modern times.

CHAPTER VIII

THE ETHICS OF DESECRATION

WITH the awakening of a world-wide interest in the tomb of Tutankhamen there has been a good deal of not altogether relevant discussion about the ethics of desecration, which is none the less unfortunate because it is inspired by ignorance of the real facts of the case. By inflaming feeling it may help to defeat the object everyone concerned is doing his utmost to achieve, that is, to secure the adequate protection and reverent treatment of the dead pharaoh and his fellow-sleepers. Hence it is necessary to put the issue in its true light.

It seems to have been overlooked by those who write about leaving the royal mummies in their own tombs that in the past only one of them was actually found in his own tomb, and that this pharaoh, Amenhotep II, was left there reposing in his own sarcophagus. It is equally important to note that it was Mr Howard Carter, who is in charge of the present

work for the late Lord Carnarvon, who was at
that time Inspector of Antiquities at Luxor and
was largely responsible for this decision.   Nor
is it any secret that those responsible for the
present work propose to leave the mummy of
Tutankhamen in the tomb, provided that the
risk of damage can be guarded against.

The issue raised by the oft-repeated protests
against desecration is complicated by the fact
that in every case the mummies of the pharaohs
were plundered and grossly maltreated by their
own subjects more than thirty centuries ago;
and, except in two or three instances, were
unceremoniously removed from their own
tombs and hidden away in any place that
happened to be convenient.

If archæologists did not open and examine
these tombs there is no doubt that in time
the native tomb-robbers of Luxor, the most
experienced members of their craft to be
found anywhere, would in time discover the
hidden tombs, plundering them and destroying
the historical evidence.   There can be no
question that the work of the archæologist
when conscientiously done saves the ancient
tombs from wilful destruction and gives the
mummies and the furniture a new lease of
assured existence.   So long as these tombs

are left alone there is always the risk that they will be desecrated at any moment.

The problem which the archæologist has to solve, once he has opened a tomb, is what is the proper course to take with reference to the mummies and the funerary equipment. It is claimed by many writers to the Press that at any rate the bodies of the kings ought to be restored.

But even if it were possible to replace the royal mummies in their own tombs, and to persuade the museums of the world to return their sarcophagi and funerary equipment, it would still be a moot point whether such procedures would save them from desecration. For, unless large sums of money are spent in equipping the tombs against the attacks of robbers and providing guards, such measures would defeat the purpose that prompted them. For the mummies would become the lure for the greed of the Theban population, which for sixty centuries and more has been habituated to tomb-robbing, and has shown little respect for the mummies of even the most famous of its rulers. In fact, the most powerful sovereigns of Egypt have suffered worst at the hands of the people of their own metropolis. The mummies of the greatest emperors and wisest

statesmen of the eighteenth dynasty, such as
Thothmes III and Amenhotep III, were
stripped and badly mutilated; and it is more
likely than not that the mummy of the famous
Hatshepsut, the Queen Elizabeth of Egyptian
history, was totally destroyed. Even when
Amenhotep II (together with the mummies
found with him) were left in his own tomb, it
was not long before the tomb was entered by
plunderers and wanton damage inflicted on
the bodies left in it. In my volume of the
Official Catalogue of the Cairo Museum,
dealing with the royal mummies, gruesome
evidence is given of the mutilation effected
upon the bodies of a prince and two princesses in
this tomb, both by ancient and modern robbers.

The moral of all this is that unless the tomb
is rendered burglar-proof, and in addition is
protected by adequate guards, it is inviting
desecration to leave the mummies in them.
Everyone immediately concerned with the problem of Tutankhamen's mummy agrees that,
if it is feasible, it should be left in its own
tomb and adequately protected there after a
thorough examination of it has been made, and
all the information as to age and infirmities which
the X rays can afford has been obtained. The
late Lord Carnarvon was strongly in favour of

this course of action, and Mr Howard Carter has always been in favour of leaving the mummies in their tombs.   But if this is done they must be adequately guarded.   For it is not an exaggeration to claim that in the past the removal of the royal mummies to the Cairo Museum saved them from destruction, or from being broken up for disposal to tourists, as in former centuries some of them were sold to druggists. For, as Sir Thomas Browne expressed it two and a half centuries ago, " The Egyptian mummies, which Cambyses or time hath spared, avarice now consumeth.   Mummy is become merchandise, Mizraim cures wounds, and Pharaoh is sold for balsams."

But, apart from such considerations, the fact has not received due acknowledgment that the archæologists who are investigating the tomb of Tutankhamen are clearly not engaged in a work of destruction or of desecration, but are striving to preserve his remains and his treasured possessions, and to secure his name and his record from the oblivion which he himself and his representatives strove so hard to avert.

The relatively slight disturbance of the antechamber holds out the prospect that the mummy also may have been spared that

wanton destruction which was the fate of so
many pharaohs of his dynasty, although it is
to be expected that the valuable gold objects
upon the body are not likely to have escaped
the plunderers.

If the mummy is found, an examination of
it by means of the X-rays will be made; but,
whatever measures are adopted for wresting
from it the story it has to tell, no one need
be anxious about its desecration. No damage
of any sort will be inflicted upon the body;
but every precaution will be taken to assure
that prolongation of its existence within its
own sarcophagus which the embalmer of
thirty-two centuries ago aimed at achieving.

In the commentary on the discoveries in
Tutankhamen's tomb I have dealt mainly with
aspects of the new revelation of Egyptian
customs and beliefs that to most readers may
seem less impressive than the dazzling display
of artistic treasures which has aroused in them
an interest in archæology.

But to the student who is interested in
tracing out the origin of the customs and
beliefs which have shaped the fabric of civilization and influenced the trends of even our own
thoughts, the objective expression of ancient
beliefs displayed in Tutankhamen's tomb is

the most important outcome of Mr Howard
Carter's discovery.

For it enables us to realize more vividly
than before the relentless and persistent logic
with which the ancient Egyptian theologian
strove by any and every device he could think
of, to make as certain as any physical or
magical procedure could make it, to give a
new lease of life or existence to the dead.
Many modern scholars object to the use of the
word logic to apply to a series of procedures
inconsistent the one with the other except in
their ultimate aim, and are constantly em-
phasizing and marvelling at their lack of cogency
and consistency. But the modern psycho-
logist has recently been insisting that we
ourselves, and, in fact, all mankind, are just
as illogical as the Ancient Egyptian priesthood.
In our everyday life we are hourly doing things
as glaringly inconsistent the one with the other
as anything that the Egyptians ever did. It
is merely that our wider acquaintance with
the nature of matter and the properties of
living creatures enables us the more readily to
hide our inconsistencies and rationalize our
statements so as to hide our ignorance and
lack of cogency.

In this connexion it is important to try and

put ourselves in the position of the theologians
of Tutankhamen's time, and ask whether it is
likely that they really imagined the ceremonial
couches to be potent to transfer the dead king
to the sky. They knew perfectly well that
the couches could not effect this physical
transference to a topographical heaven. But
long usage had accustomed them to attach a
definite symbolic meaning to the ceremonial
practice of placing the mummy of the king
upon such couches. This was supposed to
confer upon the dead king immortality and
divinity, to identify him with the sun-god Re
in the sky.

The problem which is perhaps responsible
for most disagreement between Egyptian
scholars to-day is the relationship of the two
gods Osiris and Re, with both of which the
dead king was identified as a means of attaining immortality. The obvious connecting link
between them is the rôle assigned to Horus,
who, as the son of Osiris, is charged with the
function of securing for the dead king the
same boons which he was able to confer on
Osiris. Yet as a sun-god, intimately associated
with Re, Horus could also secure for him the
solar heaven and enable him to dwell with Re,
if not be identified with him, in the sun.

There is a profound difference of opinion whether Osiris or Re was the earliest god. Philologists like Professor Breasted and Dr Blackman, who derive their knowledge from the literary texts (which, however, were not put into writing until all thought and expression were dominated by the sun cult and the Pyramid Texts were actually written by Heliopolitan priests) insist on the priority of the sun-god Re.

Ethnologists who know how relatively recent is the belief in a sky-world and in sun-worship insist upon the priority of the god Osiris, who was originally a king on earth. To my mind the whole conception of deity and the attributes of the earliest gods can be understood and explained only if we admit that Osiris was the first god and that Re acquired his reputation secondarily from Osiris.

In Tutankhamen's tomb the one idea that informed the funerary ritual and equipment was this identification with Osiris, and the solar embellishments are clearly additions to the more ancient practices. I have entered in detail into the interesting problems of the funerary couches in order to bring out in a definite and concrete form the essential meaning of the whole equipment of Tutankhamen's tomb.

What renders the obtrusiveness of the Osirian element in Tutankhamen's ritual additionally significant is the fact that he had been a worshipper of the sun's disc, the Aton, and had just been converted to that denomination of the Re-cult which was associated with Amen.   But although these different forms of the sun-cult were in turn his confessed beliefs, it is a striking demonstration of the fundamental nature of the Osirian cult that it dominates the ceremonies of Tutankhamen's death and burial.

*For Product Safety Concerns and Information please contact
our EU representative GPSR@taylorandfrancis.com Taylor & Francis
Verlag GmbH, Kaufingerstraße 24, 80331 München, Germany*

T - #0110 - 270225 - C0 - 234/156/14 - PB - 9780415652933 - Gloss Lamination